Road Cycling Spec

Advice | Sales | Service |

PINARELLO

COLNAGO®

cervélo

PARLEE

SHOWROOM
Knutsford Road, Wilmslow, Cheshire SK9 6JA
MON-SAT 09:30-18:00 | SUN-CLOSED

WWW.ROYLES.BIZ
☎ 01625 543400

WINNING TECHNOLOGY

CUBE LITENING: THE CHOICE OF REAL RIDERS

Scan this page with the free **layar app**
and enter the CUBE world!

CUBE LITENING ROAD BIKES set record marks for performance and comfort in 2013. Using Monocoque Advanced Twin Mold Technology, the high modulus carbon fibre frame is super stiff yet offers great comfort for long rides or races. That's thanks to the combination of slim Aeroflex seat stays, carbon fibre Race Flex seatposts and CSL Evo fork, which work together to damp unwanted vibrations, while high lateral stiffness at the bottom bracket guarantees optimum power transfer and acceleration. Hybrid Cable Routing delivers a clean look and great function with both mechanical electronic transmissions. Winning technology.

CUBE.EU

For more information on CUBE and our bikes please visit: www.cube.eu | info@cube-bikes.co.uk

Stay updated about all CUBE news via : **f** www.facebook.com/cubebikesuk **t** www.twitter.com/cubebikesuk

100 GREATEST MOMENTS

FROM 100 YEARS OF THE TOUR DE FRANCE

CONTENTS

139

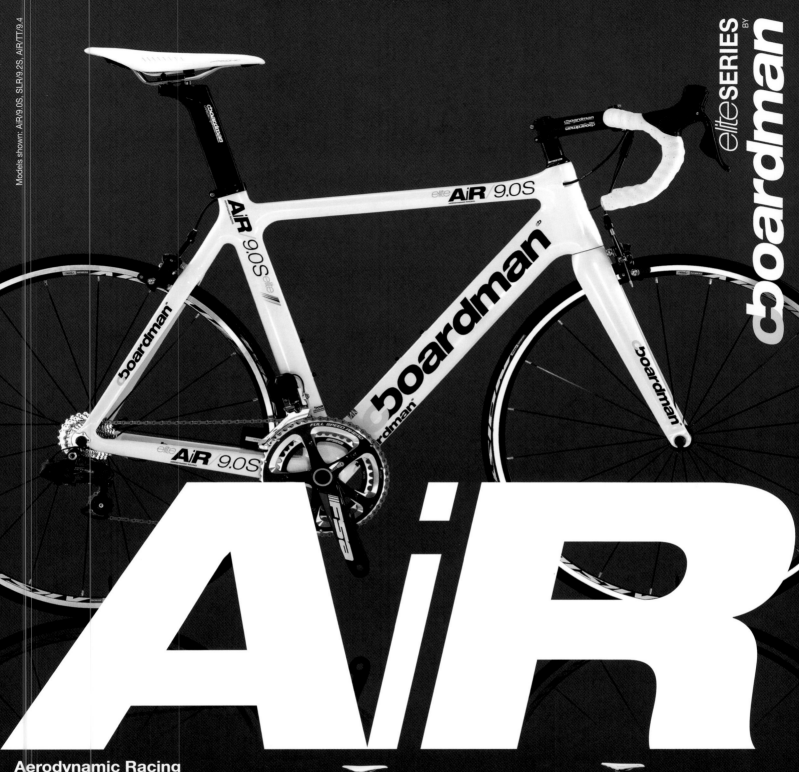

FOREWORD

 So we're here at last. I've been waiting for this moment for so long! The 100th Tour signifies nothing and everything at the same time. This should only be one Tour among all of the others, but I know very well that this won't be the case.

Each Tour is an immense event, producing many exhilarating moments, great emotion and unforgettable memories. Every single edition has contributed to the race's legendary status and grandeur.

I can remember so much about the Tour and among those memories are some that are so remarkable that they have huge significance for all fans. These are the great moments that have drawn millions of spectators to the Tour from all over the world.

I am proud to have played my part in this legendary event, and I also feel great pride when riders continue to take on this beautiful challenge and by doing so add to the glory of and love for the Tour.

RAYMOND POULIDOR

1903

The first Tour de France was an instant success. The public came out in droves to see the heroes of the road battling for victory, which eventually went to Maurice Garin

It's 3.16pm and the 60 riders who have signed up in front of the Réveil Matin set off on the first Tour de France, the start having been moved 500m along the road due to roadworks. The great adventure is under way

Maurice Garin

THE GAMBLE PAYS OFF

→ Sixty riders lined up at the start of the first Tour de France on Wednesday 1 July 1903 in front of the Au Réveil Matin auberge at Montgeron. It was 3.16pm when they set off – actually 500 metres from that point due to roadworks. The itinerary gave them plenty of causes for concern. Stage one went from Paris to Lyon and covered 467km on poorly surfaced roads. The riders were on bikes that weighed 20kg, at the very least, and didn't have a gear mechanism. They rode night and day without pacemakers; they had to carry out their own repairs; those who finished that first stage had four days to rest before setting out for Marseille, 374km away. From there they would head to Toulouse (423km), Bordeaux (268km), Nantes (425km) and finally into Paris (471km), where the official finish took place at Ville-d'Avray in front of 100,000 spectators. The riders then continued on a neutralised section of road to the track at the Parc des Princes in Paris.

Only 21 riders survived the 2,428km to the finish. The first of them was Maurice Garin, an Italian-born chimney sweep aged 32 who had taken on French nationality and set up home in Lens. He wasn't much to look at, standing a mere 1.60m tall and weighing 62kg. Yet he won in Lyon, Nantes and Paris, and took the title with an advantage of more than three hours over the next finisher, Lucien Pothier. It took Garin more than 94 hours to complete the course, meaning he spent the equivalent of four days in the saddle, averaging 25.679kmh.

The other victor was the Tour itself. It had seduced the public, who were full of enthusiasm for it and made it a huge success. The spectators, sometimes unruly in nature, thronged the roadsides. They were also very eager to get their hands on copies of daily newspaper *L'Auto*, which organised the event. That had been the goal when Géo Lefèvre had come up with the idea in the first place and seen it taken on board by Henri Desgrange (director and editor-in-chief of the paper) and Victor Goddet (managing director). Organising such an event at that time had been a real gamble – but it had paid off.

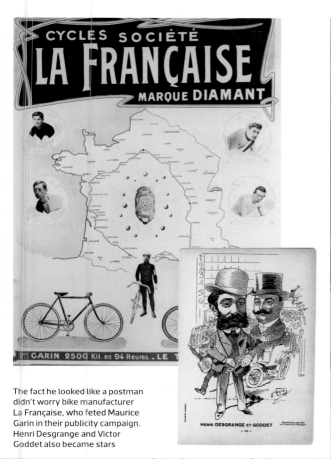

The fact he looked like a postman didn't worry bike manufacturer La Française, who feted Maurice Garin in their publicity campaign. Henri Desgrange and Victor Goddet also became stars

In Paris, Maurice Garin savours his success. With his son at his side, he has a toothpick between his lips and is wearing a blue, white and red sash. He won three of the six stages in this first edition of the race

Where it all began: outside the Au Reveil Matin on 1 July 1903. Little did these locals know what had started here with 60 riders would go on to become over the following 110 years

Henri Cornet

1904

Henri Cornet was declared the winner after the first four finishers – most notably victor Maurice Garin – had been disqualified by the French Cycling Union on 30 November 1904

Crossing the finish line in Paris, Henri Cornet was completely unaware that he had won the race. He would not find out until a few months later when the top four finishers were disqualified

'KILL THEM!' THEY CRIED

→ The introduction of fixed and random control points on the route failed to prevent riders cheating. Among the rule breakers was Frenchman Pierre Chevalier, who finished third on the first stage from Paris to Lyon but had covered part of the 467km stage in a car. During the course of the following stage, spectators got involved in the action.

On the Col de la République (1,161m), which links Saint-Étienne to the Rhône Valley, the riders got caught up in an ambush. About 200 supporters of local rider Antoine Fauré allowed their favourite to pass but threatened the rest of the peloton, chasing after them and shouting, 'Kill them!' Race officials had to fire shots in the air to guarantee the riders' safe passage. Giovanni Gerbi, who had been knocked out, had to abandon, while 1903 winner Maurice Garin received a hand injury. The tactic didn't pay off as Fauré finished fifth in Marseille, two seconds behind winner Hippolyte Aucouturier. Or at least that was the case until the first four riders were disqualified at the end of November as the sport put its house back in order.

1905

Already the winner of Paris-Roubaix, Frenchman Louis Trousselier added the Tour de France to his CV – but it wasn't an easy ride

Louis Trousselier

WITH THE PERMISSION OF THE ARMY

→ Louis Trousselier had to overcome two major obstacles at the start of the Tour. The first was thousands of tacks that had been scattered on the road by someone protesting against the race. There were 125kg of them in total. They resulted in every rider puncturing apart from one (Jean-Baptiste Dortignacq).

The second was more personal. To start the race, 'Trou-Trou', as he was known, had to get permission from the French army. He managed to get temporary leave, but not for long enough to complete the race. The first stage was rained off, but then Trousselier won in Nancy to take first place in the overall standings, which were decided on points. The army's hierarchy were swayed by his success and allowed him to extend his adventure. By way of thanks, he would win four more stages and the overall title before returning to barracks.

DEVILISHLY GOOD DEALS AT WIGGLE.COM!

HUGE SAVINGS ON THE BIGGEST BRANDS AND PRODUCTS, EACH DAY OF LE TOUR

Le Tour de wiggle

DI2 ELECTRONIC GEARS!
Verenti Revelation Ultegra
See the new range of
Verenti Bikes online now

SRAM Red
Doubletap Shifters
The latest SRAM Components
always in stock

NEW SEASON CLOTHING!
Castelli Velocissimo
DS Short Sleeve Jersey
The latest range online now

passion | performance | perfection

wiggle

SAFE AND SECURE SHOPPING ∞ SUPERB VALUE ∞ FREE DELIVERY ∞ WORLDWIDE SERVICE

*Terms and conditions apply. Visit www.wiggle.com for latest prices, promotions and free delivery conditions.

FASTER THAN A SPEEDING CAR

→ The mountains first appeared in the Tour in 1905 when the riders tackled the Ballon d'Alsace, where René Pottier first came to the fore. Heading towards the same climb the following year on the Nancy-Dijon stage, the 27-year-old Frenchman was leading the race, and he extended his advantage by attacking and dropping his rivals one by one. At the summit he had a lead of 4m 30secs on Georges Passerieu and just as much on race director Henri Desgrange's car, which couldn't cope with his acceleration either. This despite the fact that Pottier had climbed the Ballon at an average of 20kmh.

When he was back on the flat, Pottier pulled off an exceptional feat: he kept going with his solo break, which extended to 215km by the

1906

Thanks to his exceptional ability as a climber, René Pottier crushed his rivals early on in the race and went on to finish a convincing winner in Paris

time he reached Dijon, where he finished more than 47 minutes ahead. Having taken back-to-back stage wins, he immediately added two more in Grenoble and Nice. The Tour was over. Sadly, the future of the Tour's first great climber was not a happy one: he hung himself on 25 January 1907, apparently due to his wife falling in love with another man.

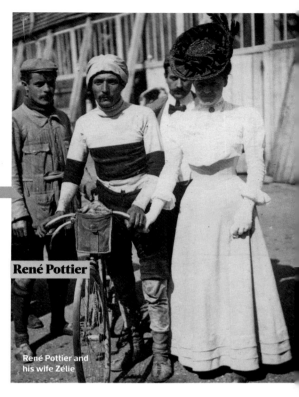

René Pottier

René Pottier and his wife Zélie

1907

Émile Georget seemed set to win the race when he was disqualified in Bayonne following an illegal bike change. He quit with his team, leaving Lucien Petit-Breton to profit by winning the Tour

The start of the 11th stage in Bordeaux

THE TOUR GOES ABROAD

→ For the first time the Tour went abroad for a stage finish. It took place in Metz, which had been annexed by Germany in 1870. In Metz, Count Johann Friedrich Alexander von Zeppelin-Aschhausen, president of the Bezirk Lothringen (Lorraine) region (and nephew of the inventor of the airship), welcomed the hero of the day, Louis Trousselier.

Or at least he thought he had, because the judges, believing they had made a mistake in a close finish, then decided Émile Georget had won the stage, only to revise that verdict by eventually making the two men joint winners.

The key thing was that the German administrators of Lorraine cooperated on all matters, allowing not only the riders passage through the border, but also the amateur riders accompanying them. It was the French who imposed pernickety controls, insisting that all of the bikes were marked with a lead stamp. Subsequently, the first part of the third stage between Metz and Belfort had to be neutralised – at four in the morning – so that all of the stamps could be checked.

PETIT-BRETON BECOMES A GREAT

→ He was called Lucien Mazan and until the age of 20 he lived in Buenos Aires, which explains his nickname, 'The Argentine'. Yet he didn't make his name using the surname Mazan, but by adopting the pseudonym 'Breton', which later became 'Petit-Breton', to hide the fact he was racing from his father. The pseudonym harked back to his Breton origins.

As elegant on the bike as off it, Mazan was a model of consistency and perfectly exploited the rules, which still decided the race on points. He finished well up on every stage, even in Bordeaux, despite puncturing and coming 10th. Apart from that setback, he finished second three times, third five times and won five stages, leaving all the rest for his team-mates to share between them: François Faber won four, Georges Passerieu three, Jean-Baptiste Dortignacq and Georges Paulmier one each. The 26-year-old had shown he understood the race perfectly, to the point where he even designated his successor, François Faber.

1908
Lucien Petit-Breton, leader of a Peugeot team that fills the first four places in the overall standings, becomes the first rider to win the Tour twice

Lucien Petit-Breton

1909
A foreign rider wins the Tour for the first time. The race is won by the strapping Luxembourger François Faber, who dominates both tactically and, at 91kg, physically

François Faber

WINNING A STAGE ON FOOT

→ It was 1 August, but the rain hammered down as Jean Alavoine pushed his bike. Earlier on what was the 14th and final stage, covering 251km between Caen and Paris, he had made a solo attack. However, about 10km from the finish in the Parc des Princes he fell and broke his chain. He had no other option but to continue on foot, either pushing his bike or carrying it on his shoulder, but always running as he did so.

It was in this unusual manner that the champion of France won the most improbable of stage victories, his second in this race after a previous success in Toulouse. He would finish 6m 30secs up on Louis Trousselier and 6m 36secs ahead of François Faber, who had so wanted to win this stage to add to the prestige of his overall victory. Jean Alavoine was then just 21 and would go on to win 17 Tour stages between 1909 and 1923, which was a record. He did win most of them on the bike…

The first rider to the top of the Tourmalet, Octave Lapize swapped between walking and riding to reach that objective. Only Gustave Garrigou remained in the saddle all the way to the summit

1910

Thanks to a heroic performance in the Pyrenees on the occasion of the first appearance of the high mountains in the Tour, Octave Lapize not only won the race but also claimed legendary status

Octave Lapize

A GIANT OF THE TOUR EMERGES

'You are all criminals!' yelled Octave Lapize at the Tour organisers, leaving no doubt about his feelings. There were still 150km ahead on the 10th stage between Luchon and Bayonne, which extended to 326km in total, and the Frenchman had had enough. Together with Gustave Garrigou, he had already led the race over the Peyresourde (1,569m) and Aspin (1,489m) passes, and he had suffered on the slopes of the next monstrous climb on the route. The Tourmalet not only topped out at 2,115m, but in 1910 the road over it was impassable for vehicles and frequented by herds of livestock.

The idea of heading deep into the Pyrenees and putting its highest summits on the itinerary was born in the – some would say slightly deranged – mind of one of Henri Desgrange's closest colleagues, Alphonse Steinès. He had come to the area a few months earlier on reconnaissance and had crossed the Tourmalet on foot before disappearing behind a snowdrift

as fatigue overtook him. That experience didn't prevent him from judging the Tourmalet an ideal test for the riders. And so the giant mountains made their first appearance in the race.

Lapize switched between walking and riding. He was cursing but still led the race over the summit and continued on to tackle the remaining challenges of the day, notably the Col d'Aubisque (1,709m). Behind him, it was carnage: in Bayonne, where he claimed the stage more than two hours after the predicted finishing time, François Faber was 10 minutes behind, Gustave Garrigou almost an hour. The last riders would finish seven-and-a-half hours after Lapize. They were outside the time limit, like plenty of others. Desgrange, being the gentleman he was, allowed them all to continue.

The introduction to the Tour de France route of the Pyrenees in 1910 and the Alps the following year led to the birth of a new breed of rider – the climbers, for whom the fans reserve the greatest adulation

THE KINGS OF THE MOUNTAINS

Whether known as 'The Angel of the Mountains', 'The Eagle of Toledo' or by some other nickname, climbers have always received a great deal of respect. In this case, the names refer to Luxembourg's Charly Gaul and Spain's Federico Bahamontes, respectively, and honour their magnificence. Even five-time winners of the Tour tend to received a less elegant tag: Eddy Merckx was 'The Cannibal', while Bernard Hinault was 'The Badger', although he was undoubtedly the best climber of his generation.

The reason for this – and it's a bit of a paradox – is that climbers tend to be weak in other areas. While Merckx, Hinault, Indurain and even Anquetil never had rivals able to shake them off in the mountains as they were racking up Tour victories, they were never considered great climbers. To be recognised as a climber a rider has to be capable not only of stunning attacks, thrilling breaks or taking prestigious victories, but equally to be incapable of anything else but that.

However, some of them have managed to move beyond the role of troublemaker that seven-time King of the Mountains Richard Virenque played to perfection. These riders have managed to take the greatest prize in spite of their gift for climbing. Among them are Charly Gaul (1958), Federico Bahamontes (1959), Lucien Van Impe (1976), Marco Pantani (1998) and before them Gino Bartali (1938 and 1948) and Fausto Coppi (1949 and 1952). This was well after the time when the classic Pyrenean stage comprising the Soulor, Aubisque and Tourmalet tended to almost systematically decide the winner of the Tour.

Charly Gaul in front of a majestic backdrop on the eighth stage of the 1955 Tour de France between Thonon and Briançon. The Luxembourger would scatter his rivals and win the stage

Throughout his career, Richard Virenque
(seen here in 1997) collected polka-
dot jerseys. He won the best climber
classification on seven occasions:
1994-1997, 1999, 2003 and 2004

The great Tour champions have been able to master the climbers in the mountains: on this occasion, Miguel Indurain is making life tough for Claudio Chiappucci, King of the Mountains champion in 1991 and 1992

Italy's Fausto Coppi (in the background) is finding it hard to keep a check on Frenchman Jean Robic, who's not wearing his usual cyclocross leather helmet. Anything can happen in the mountains

Federico Bahamontes built his 1959 victory around his successes in the mountains. Standing out on the climbs was nothing new for the Spaniard, who was crowned the race's best climber six times: 1954, 1958 and 1959-1962

Marco Pantani triumphs at Plateau de Beille and moves himself back into the fight for overall victory. The 1998 Tour would see the Italian consecrated as a cycling great as he completed the Giro-Tour double

Winner of the Tour on two occasions 10 years apart (1938 and 1948), the Italian Gino Bartali always shone in the Alps. Here he is seen setting the pace through the Casse Déserte section of the Col d'Izoard

Winner of the 10th stage of the 1952 Tour between Lausanne and Alpe d'Huez (and seen here accompanied by Jean Robic), Italy's Fausto Coppi would go on to defend his yellow jersey by triumphing the next day at Sestrières

Bernard Thévenet and Lucien Van Impe often found themselves alone at the front of the Tour. In 1975 the Belgian Van Impe had his sights set on the mountains title (he won it six times between 1971 and 1983), while the Frenchman Thévenet was eyeing overall victory

There was a change of emphasis for Van Impe in 1976, when he rode to win the Tour rather than just the mountains title. Wearing the yellow jersey, he had to counter the attacks of his closest rival, Dutchman Joop Zoetemelk (right)

Gustave Garrigou

1911

An extremely sudden and suspect weakness on the part of Paul Duboc left the way clear for Gustave Garrigou (second in 1907 and 1909, third in 1910), who finally finished on the top step of the podium

In feed zones, riders needed be cautious of overeager hands... Duboc seemed to pay the price of not being cautious enough

'HAVE I BEEN POISONED?'

Paul Duboc negotiated the Alps perfectly, notably when finishing second behind Émile Georget on the tortuous fifth stage between Chamonix and Grenoble, which featured the Aravis (1,498m), Télégraphe (1,670m), Lautaret (2,058m) and, above all, the Galibier for the first time in Tour history. He went on to win the eighth stage in Perpignan, then the ninth in Luchon. He was beginning to threaten leader Gustave Garrigou.

Even better, on the 10th stage to Bayonne, the 27-year-old Frenchman led over the Peyresourde and Aspin, and looked full of energy on the Tourmalet. Writing his daily column for *L'Auto*, Henri Desgrange judged him to be 'shimmering with brio, fluidity and ability'. However, a few kilometres further on, on the Aubisque, Desgrange came across Duboc sitting at the side of the road 'making fearful retching noises, turning green with nausea, affected by terrible diarrhoea and vomiting painfully'.

An hour and a quarter passed before he could get back in the saddle and continue to finish 20th in Bayonne, more than three hours down

on the winner. He lost the stage and the Tour, which went to Garrigou. What had happened? It now seems to have been established that a water bottle handed to him at a feed station contained something that could be at the very least described as doubtful. An inquiry was opened, and the names of several suspects circulated, but nothing would ever be proven.

'Have I been poisoned?' wondered Duboc, who finished second in Paris. 'I don't know and I probably never will. All that I do know is that Garrigou is incapable of such an act.'

DEFRAYE CLAIMS BELGIUM'S FIRST WIN

→ For the first time, the race was opened up to teams backed by bike manufacturers. Ten teams of five took to the start, but Henri Desgrange kept a close eye on them: cycling, he insisted, was a sport of individuals, so team-mates helping each other was out of the question. Yet it wasn't team interests that were the deciding factor, but national interests.

There were 18 Belgians at the start, spread among the trade teams, but they set about ensuring that their national champion, a certain Odile Defraye, made off with the main prize. Disheartened, Octave Lapize abandoned in protest on the Col du Portet d'Aspet (stage nine)

1912

Called up to the Tour to help Garrigou win a second title, Belgian debutant Odile Defraye ended up taking the crown after crushing his leader and everyone else

and his team-mates didn't start the next stage.

A number of complaints were made against Defraye: for missing a secret control point, for taking a 150m shortcut on the Galibier, and for being paced by compatriot René Vandenberghe, who rode for the rival Thomann team. But none of them prevented him winning. The result was that Belgium could celebrate its first Tour de France success.

Odile Defraye

Odile Defraye (centre) doesn't look like a champion in waiting. But looks can be deceiving

1913

The return to a classification based on time changed nothing as far as the result was concerned because once again a Belgian took the title. On this occasion it was Philippe Thys, the king of the Pyrenees

VIE AU GRAND AIR

NUMÉRO SPÉCIAL · LE TOUR DE FRANCE CYCLISTE

CHRISTOPHE FORGES HIS LEGEND

→ On the morning of the sixth stage from Bayonne to Luchon, Eugène Christophe was lying second overall, 4m 55secs down on Belgian Odile Defraye. However, Defraye would soon crack and abandon the race, leaving the way open to the Frenchman, who led over the Col d'Aubisque and set about the ascent of the Tourmalet with only Philippe Thys alongside. On the descent he collided with a car and broke the forks on his bike.

He walked for 14km with his bike on his back. In the valley, he reached the village of Sainte-Marie-de-Campan and found a forge where he was able to borrow the tools he needed to repair his forks – riders weren't allowed to receive any outside help at all.

Four hours later, Christophe finally completed the repair under the watchful eyes of two race judges. He jumped back on board his bike, climbed the Aspin and Peyresourde and reached Luchon three hours and 50 minutes behind Thys, who had won the stage and would go on to win the Tour. As for Eugène Christophe, he would finish seventh in Paris.

1914

The race saw Belgium claim a third consecutive title as Philippe Thys retained his crown. Despite winning just a single stage, he led from start to finish

Three Tour winners on the attack: Faber, Garrigou and Thys climb the Col d'Allos

Philippe Thys

LAST TOUR BEFORE 'THE BIG MATCH'

With just two days to the finish, Philippe Thys was a happy and relaxed man. He held an advantage of 31m 50secs over second-placed Henri Pélissier going into the 14th and penultimate stage between Longwy and Dunkirk. He had crushed his rivals in the Pyrenees, and was comfortably heading towards his second consecutive victory when he collided with an amateur cyclist. He was left with a broken wheel, although it didn't prove too serious as he managed to finish third in Dunkirk in the same time as the first two riders, François Faber and Henri Pélissier. However, because he had forgotten to report to the judges that his hub had broken following its repair, the race commissaires hit him with a 30-minute penalty.

His comfortable lead disappeared and would end up being the narrowest margin recorded between the winner and the runner-up to date. The Belgian's lead was just 1m 50secs when the final stage finished in Paris.

But this year's Tour de France was already being overshadowed. When Thys celebrated victory in Paris on 26 July, Europe was about to explode. On 3 August, Germany declared war on Belgium and France. The Great War – which Henri Desgrange called 'the big match' in a headline in *L'Auto*, before going on to enlist at the age of 50 – would cost the lives of nine million people. Among them were three Tour winners – François Faber, Lucien Petit-Breton and Octave Lapize – and about 50 Tour riders.

THE GOLDEN FLEECE

The statistics speak volumes: of the 127 riders registered for the first post-war Tour, no fewer than 59 did not start, largely due to the lack of equipment, particularly tyres. Of the 68 starters, only 41 reached Le Havre at the end of the first stage and just 27 got to Cherbourg at the end of the second. The peloton that arrived in Paris on 27 July was very scrawny indeed, numbering just 11 riders. Only 10 of those would end up being classified following the later disqualification of Paul Duboc, who had got into a car on the final stage to catch up with the peloton.

The main cause of this carnage was terrible weather as the race was hit by freezing cold and torrential rain. But the state of the roads didn't help either. There were numerous punctures, broken bikes and a severe lack of equipment with which to carry out repairs.

'The Old Gaul', 35-year-old Eugène Christophe, was the most severely affected.

1919

Firmin Lambot continued Belgium's winning run at the Tour de France. Partly due to some ill-fortune that befell Eugène Christophe, Lambot finished in Paris wearing the yellow jersey

Well clear at the head of the standings with two stages remaining, he started the first of them with a 28-minute advantage over Belgium's Firmin Lambot, but was delayed when his forks broke between Metz and Dunkirk. Just as he had done in 1913, he repaired his bike but lost almost two-and-a-half hours. Lambot inherited the yellow jersey, which now marked out the race leader. Eugène Christophe had been the first one to wear the golden fleece on the 11th stage between Grenoble and Geneva.

Firmin Lambot

1920

Already the winner in 1913 and 1914, Philippe Thys became the first man to win the Tour three times as the Belgian domination continued – they filled the first seven places

Between Nice and Grenoble the Belgians put on a demonstration of their power

FETED BY THE PUBLIC

The fans at the Parc des Princes carried him shoulder-high in triumph: Honoré Barthélémy was the true hero of the day. This wasn't due to fact he had finished eighth overall and first Frenchman, but because the 29-year-old Parisian had shown extraordinary courage.

During the eighth stage between Perpignan and Aix-en-Provence, Barthélémy had crashed heavily. Groggy, bleeding and unable to bend his back, he was scarcely able to get back on his bike. He rode the rest of the stage with his body stiffening up and his head hanging down, suffering like a martyr. His face was burning with pain. At the finish, the doctor's diagnosis was severe: he had dislocated a wrist, broken a shoulder and burst an eye.

His eye socket plugged with cotton wool to prevent infection, he completed the final seven stages and 2,500km of the race, arriving in triumph in Paris. In 1921, with a glass eye fitted, Barthélémy won the Geneva-Strasbourg stage and finished on the third step of the podium.

A VICTORY TOO EASILY WON

→ Henri Desgrange was angry. When Léon Scieur and Honoré Barthélémy escaped on the 12th stage from Geneva to Strasbourg and were joined by Hector Heusghem, the Tour director had huge admiration for the three men's courage, but he wasn't aware what was going on behind them. It was when he found out that he became angry, because nothing was happening behind them. The gap widened between the three leaders and the peloton, but still no one reacted. At the finish it had reached almost 28 minutes.

Desgrange was ruthless in his response. He penalised Belgians Louis Mottiat and Firmin Lambot (who had finished sixth and 11th respectively in Strasbourg) for a lack of fight by relegating them to the last places on the stage.

1921

Like Firmin Lambot, Léon Scieur hailed from the Flemish village of Florennes. He won the Tour easily after his rivals yielded to his superiority too early

Two days later, he ensured that the elite and second-class riders started the stage at different times. However, that still didn't rouse the supposed stars from their lethargy. They finished the stage between Strasbourg and Metz 45 minutes behind a trio of amateurs – Félix Sellier, Victor Lenaers and Joël Muller.

Léon Scieur

1922

Three years after his first success, 36-year-old Belgian Firmin Lambot became the oldest winner in Tour history and also picked up a new nickname – 'Lucky'

Firmin Lambot

THE MARK OF A CHAMPION

→ Philippe Thys won five stages; Jean Alavoine took three in succession at Bayonne, Luchon and Perpignan. As for Firmin Lambot, he didn't win any, but he took advantage of circumstances.

Thys shone in the Pyrenees but broke a wheel. Eugène Christophe seemed a solid leader, but blew up unexpectedly on the seventh stage before finally being ejected from the battle for overall victory on the Galibier when his forks broke yet again. Jean Alavoine succeeded him in the yellow jersey, holding a 29-minute lead over Lambot at Briançon, but he was suddenly hit by a string of punctures – he lost 37 minutes on the 12th stage, 23 on the 13th and 16 on the 14th to drop him out of contention.

Finally, it fell to Hector Heusghem to take up the running as the potential winner. But he damaged his bike, swapped it for another when it could have been repaired and picked up a one-hour penalty as a result. That incident took place on the 13th stage and Lambot, who was wearing number 13, pulled on the yellow jersey, which he hadn't been expecting at the age of 36, and held it all the way to Paris.

Firmin Lambot (leading) would take the yellow jersey from Hector Heusghem (behind) as a result of a one-hour penalty imposed on Heusghem for changing his bike

On the Aubisque, Henri Pélissier leads Robert Jacquinot. But it was on 14 July that the Pélissier brothers blew the race wide open. It was then that Henri kissed Francis (below)

LA BICYCLETTE CHRISTOPHE
BOYAUX W. RUSSELL
est aussi populaire que LUI
CONSTRUITE sur les DONNÉES de CHRISTOPHE

1923

Finally, a Frenchman finished in yellow in Paris! Ably assisted by his younger brother Francis, Henri Pélissier roused the public with his performances and panache

Henri Pélissier

THOROUGHBREDS OUTPACE THE WORKHORSES

→ The 1923 race didn't feature trainers, support cars or soigneurs, although some back-up was available at start/finish towns. The bikes were stamped so that they could not be swapped, but for the first time the rules allowed for components to be changed. Was this a mere detail? No.

Take, for example, Eugène Christophe. What would his CV have looked like if that rule had been in place when he broke his forks on three different Tours? Falling just about halfway between the appearance of the freewheel (in 1912) and the rules being relaxed to allow the use of derailleurs (in 1937), this innovation was not quite as revolutionary as those developments, but was more a simple evolution as the race progressed. It perhaps explained what François Mercier described in *L'Auto* as 'the splendid revenge of the hares of the road over hard and durable men'. Writer André Reuze was more lyrical, evoking images of 'thoroughbreds' and 'workhorses'.

Out went the likes of Lambot, Thys and Scieur, Belgians who were race-hardened but ageing and profited from the misfortunes of others, particularly when it came to equipment. In their place came riders with panache. The proof? In Nice, as he prepared to head into the Alps, Henri Pélissier was lying third overall, 29m 52secs down on Ottavio Bottecchia, the first Italian to wear the yellow jersey. But this Tour was far from over. In two days, thanks to the assistance he got from his brother, Pélissier led over the Allos, Izoard, Galibier and Aravis passes, winning in both Briançon and Geneva to turn the classification on its head. After that masterstroke, he now led Bottecchia by 29m 12secs. The Tour had been decided.

The bicycle has undergone an extraordinary transformation from the rudimentary bikes of 1903 that weighed 20 kilos to the incredibly sophisticated machines of the 21st century

THE STARS OF THE SHOW

→ The rules of the International Cycling Union (UCI) now oblige riders to use a bike weighing at least 6.8kg. Some bikes are randomly selected at stage finishes to verify that they conform to the rules. What would the heroes of 1903, who had to race on bikes weighing three times that, think about this? That year's winner, Maurice Garin, would be amazed by the equipment being used in the 21st century: frames made out of carbon fibre or titanium, designed with cutting-edge technology, which extends to the bars and even the brake levers to reduce wind resistance as much as possible. He would be astounded by the sight of disc wheels, stunned by aero helmets, taken aback by the systems used to fix shoes to pedals, and intrigued by the bar extensions that have been inherited from triathlon. And it would probably take him some time to understand that the fixed wheel is now a thing of the past at the Tour and that they have not only been replaced by derailleurs, but that some of those systems now operate electronically.

He would no doubt be equally shocked by the earpieces that allow the modern rider to receive information from his directeur sportif, especially as he was competing at the Tour in an era when Henri Desgrange was adamant that cycling must be a sport for individuals rather than teams.

The Tour de France has changed profoundly. The equipment on which the riders perform nowadays no longer has anything in common with that used in Garin's heroic era.

When he quit racing, 1911 Tour winner Gustave Garrigou, seen posing in this coloured-in picture, became an ironmonger

A little bag for two water bottles, a pump on the frame and rudimentary brakes and toe-clips. With two tubes wrapped around his shoulders, Octave Lapize looks very much the part in 1910

Matching socks for riders on the Jean Delatour team in 2003 (top). Their shoes have nothing in common with those used by Rémy Raoul of the South-East team in 1947, when he is seen in action on the second stage from Nice to Marseille (bottom left). And they have even less in common with these hastily redesigned shoes with the toe-clip cut off at the front that belong to a rider in the 1964 Tour, who crashed on the Toulon-Montpellier stage and, to provide himself with a degree of comfort, hasn't hesitated in adapting his equipment (bottom right)

Over the course of a century, components (such as brakes, clipless pedals instead of toe-clips, and wheels) have evolved considerably. One constant remains: to get anywhere on the Tour de France, all riders have to have gear sprockets on their rear wheel

All riders have problems with their equipment. Those affected here are Antonin Magne in 1931 (top left), Fausto Coppi in 1952, Raymond Poulidor in 1975 and Georges Laloup in 1930 (bottom left to right). Such issues are inevitable even though mechanics like these on the 1929 and 1922 Tours (top right and above) are employed to check everything over

On the 7.3km prologue in Rouen, which hosted
the start of the 1997 Tour, Chris Boardman
demonstrates his qualities as a rouleur on his
futuristic Eddy Merckx bike. It's very different
to the bikes used by the sport's pioneers

During the 14th stage of the 1947 Tour between Carcassonne and Luchon, Frenchman Albert Bourlon heads for victory on what's set to be the longest solo escape in the race's history: he will end up spending 253km on the drops on what is by now quite a light bike, but is still quite uncomfortable

Cyclist
The thrill of the ride

☑ **YES! I would like to get the first 3 issues of *Cyclist* for just £5 (worth £15).** I understand that if I am not entirely satisfied, I can write to cancel at any time during the 3-issue trial period and I will pay no more than the £5 already debited. If I do decide to continue receiving *Cyclist*, I don't have to do anything – my subscription will continue at the low rate selected below.

YOUR DETAILS:

Mr/Mrs/Ms/Other: _____ Forename: _____

Surname: _____

Address: _____

_____

_____

Postcode: _____

Country: _____ Year of birth: _____

Daytime phone No: _____

Mobile phone No: _____

Email: _____

DIRECT DEBIT PAYMENT:

☐ **Print + Digital edition** – 3 issues for £5, then £31.99 every 6 issues
(Saving 10% on the shop price and 90% on digital access)

☐ **Print only edition** – 3 issues for £5, then £26.99 every 6 issues
(Saving 10% on the shop price)

Dennis — Instruction to your Bank or Building Society to pay by Direct Debit — **DIRECT Debit**

Name and full postal address of your Bank or Building Society

To the manager: Bank name _____

Address _____

Postcode _____

Account in the name(s) of _____

Branch sort code ☐☐ ☐☐ ☐☐

Bank/Building Society account number ☐☐☐☐☐☐☐☐

Originator's Identification Number

| 7 | 2 | 4 | 6 | 8 | 0 |

Instructions to your Bank or Building Society
Please pay Dennis Publishing Ltd. Direct Debits from the account detailed in this instruction subject to the safeguards assured by the Direct Debit Guarantee. I understand that this instruction may remain with Dennis Publishing Ltd. and, if so, details will be passed electronically to my Bank/Building Society.

Signature(s) _____

Date _____

Banks and building societies may not accept Direct Debit instructions for some types of account

---

Return this order form to:

FREEPOST RLZS-ETGT-BCZR, *Cyclist*, 800 Guillat Avenue, Kent Science Park, Sittingbourne ME9 8GU (NO STAMP REQUIRED)

Quote offer code G1302B for Print + Digital **OR** quote offer code G1302P for Print only

---

THE PRINT PACKAGE:

Get 3 beautiful printed issues direct to your door for just £5!

● FREE delivery

● Exclusive subscriber covers

● Save 10% on the shop price if you choose to continue your subscription

Visit **dennismags.co.uk/Cyclist**
and enter offer code **G1302P**

THE WHOLE PACKAGE:

Get 3 print and digital editions for just £5!

● FREE delivery

● Exclusive subscriber covers

● Access to our stunning app – get all our great content on the move!

● Save 90% on the standard digital subscription rate

● Save 10% on thr printed edition shop price if you choose to continue your subscription

Visit **dennismags.co.uk/Cyclist**
and enter offer code **G1302B**

Get 3 issues
FOR JUST £5

and receive every issue of *Cyclist* **before** it's available in the shops

Cyclist is a celebration of the freedom to explore and the gear that makes road cycling so special.

YOUR GREAT DEAL:

- Get 3 issues for £5
- SAVE 10% on the shop price if you choose to continue your print subscription and SAVE 90% on digital access
- FREE delivery direct to your home
- Exclusive subscriber only collectors' edition covers

The thrill of the ride

Cyclist
For the ROAD

Short and Steep
Cyclist takes on Europe's toughest gradients

Rethink your winter training

Team Sky's new kit revealed

The future of brake systems is here

Marianne Vos
Best cyclist in the world?

ISSUE 5 ● MAR 2013 ● £5

Subscribe today by calling
0844 245 6929

Or visit : **dennismags.co.uk/Cyclist**

PRISONERS OF THE ROAD

→ Henri and Francis Pélissier quickly realised that the Italian Ottavio Bottecchia would be untouchable. During the third stage, they seized on the pretext of a minor point in the rules – which they made out was abusive – to quit the race, together with their team-mate Maurice Ville. Sat in the Café de la Gare in Coutances, the three riders noticed renowned journalist Albert Londres coming in. He was the special envoy on the Tour for *Le Petit Parisien*, a rival to *L'Auto*, which organised the event.

They sat down with him at a table. 'You've got no idea what the Tour de France is like,' said Henri. 'It's a calvary. However, there are only 14 Stations of the Cross, while we have to go through 15. They wouldn't put mules through what they do to us.' Then they tipped out their bags, in a very literal sense, revealing cocaine

('for the eyes') and pills that they took 'to keep them going'. The article was published under the headline: 'The prisoners of the road'. The titled echoed that of the best-seller Albert Londres had just published. He had been writing about prisoners sentenced to hard labour in Cayenne.

1924

Having worn the yellow jersey from the first day to the last, Ottavio Bottecchia was crowned the first Italian winner of the Tour de France following the decision of the Pélissier brothers to quit

The Pélissier brothers and Maurice Ville in the Café de la Gare in Coutances

Ottavio Bottecchia

Bottecchia (right) and Van Dam

1925

There wasn't a single Frenchman in the top 10 at the end of the second Tour won by Italy's Ottavio Bottecchia, who on this occasion had to 'loan' his yellow jersey out to Adelin Benoît

THE BENEVOLENT DICTATOR

→ As in 1924, Ottavio Bottecchia won the first stage in Le Havre and the final one in Paris. As in 1924, he won twice in between, in Bordeaux and in Bayonne, following victories in Luchon and Perpignan the previous year. It seemed that 'The Woodcutter of Friuli', a mason by trade, was laying the foundations for a string of successes. However, this turned out to be his final one.

At 31 and on his third appearance in the race, Bottecchia had learned everything he needed to know about the Tour de France. He didn't make any of the mistakes he had committed in 1923 and knew how to manage the race better than he had in 1924. He was more mature, more solid. His domination was absolute, although he never humiliated his rivals. He was a benevolent dictator who enjoyed seeing his faithful lieutenant, Lucien Buysse, finish second.

Did the old guard realise their time had passed? Eugène Christophe, Philippe Thys, Henri Pélissier, Jean Alavoine, Louis Mottiat and Hector Heusghem all bid farewell to the Tour…

Between Luchon and Bayonne, nothing could stop Lucien Buysse

1926

Thirty-three-year-old Belgian Lucien Buysse took the title with a margin of an hour and 22 minutes over the runner-up thanks to his all-round strength and his exploits in the Pyrenees

TOUR DE FRANCE 1926
(CHALLENGE de RÉGULARITÉ)
1er
Alcyon
(Pneus DUNLOP)
APRÈS AVOIR GAGNÉ 7 ÉTAPES

Lucien Buysse

WATER, WATER EVERYWHERE

→ Henri Desgrange wanted to spice up his race by shortening the distance the riders had to cover before they reached the mountains and cut the number of long and flat stages that he regarded as soporific. In addition, for the first time the race started in the provinces rather than in Paris. The riders travelled in a special train from the capital, and it was Évian-les-Bains that received the honour of hosting what was not yet called the Grand Départ.

At the same time, although Desgrange was keeping it quiet, the initiative was designed to boost the race organiser's coffers by honouring a deal agreed in 1925 with Évian water. The town

also hosted the finish of the 15th stage and the start of the 16th. The route, the longest in history at 5,745km, featured no fewer than 10 bunch sprints. Everything was decided, as it often has been, on the fearsome Pyrenean stage between Bayonne and Luchon, which was made even more terrible by apocalyptic weather conditions. There was plenty of water – although not of the mineral variety – and snow as well. Some riders admitted that they had to urinate on their freewheel to defrost it.

Unhindered by these concerns, the Belgian Lucien Buysse built up huge time gaps, which he increased even further the following day.

1927

Eighteen years after François Faber, another Luxembourger won the Tour. In fact, 28-year-old Nicolas Frantz did even more than that: he made his rivals look ridiculous

FRANTZ STROLLS OVER THE SUMMITS

Throughout his career as the Tour boss, Henri Desgrange searched for ways to increase the amount of action in the race, and in his eyes 1926 was a failure. The 1927 edition saw a return to the usual habit of starting in Paris, but featured an innovative route: there were more stages (24) but they were shorter, there were fewer rest days (7), every one of them

following a big mountain stage, while all of the flat stages (16) began with teams starting separately. The teams set out one by one at 15-minute intervals.

The early part of the Tour suggested a French renaissance as Francis Pélissier and Ferdinand Le Drogo both wore the yellow jersey, the rest was nothing less than a demonstration on the

part of Nicolas Frantz. In Paris, the gaps he had built up in the mountains were immense: second-placed Maurice De Waele was almost two hours behind; the fifth-placed rider was 4h 45mins; the 10th-placed more than seven hours down; and the last finisher was more than 30 hours back! Frantz was quite simply the best rider in the best team.

Nicolas Frantz

Nicolas Frantz

1928

Having worn the yellow jersey from the first day to the last, Nicolas Frantz defended his title in spite of an accident three days from the finish that could have cost him everything

YELLOW FROM START TO FINISH

Nicolas Frantz won the first stage and the last, and in between these two successes he claimed three others – in Sables-d'Olonne (stage 6), Nice (stage 12) and Metz (stage 18) – at intervals that were so regular that you could be forgiven for wondering if they were premeditated. Even better, though, was the fact that Frantz wore the yellow jersey from start to finish. He was unstoppable.

However, the Luxembourger did give everyone a fright three days from the finish. During the 19th stage from Metz to Charleville, his bike broke a third of the way into the 159km stage. He quickly jumped onto a new bike, but it was too small for him – it was a lady's bike – and he had a very uncomfortable ride over the final 100km. He only finished 42nd that day, 37m 51secs behind the stage winner, France's Marcel Huot, and, more importantly, 27m 36secs behind his most dangerous rival in the overall classification, André Leducq. In Paris, the gap between the two men in the final standings was, consequently, 'only' 50 minutes.

A CORPSE RIDES TO VICTORY

During the 14th stage between Nice and Grenoble, Maurice De Waele was a very fragile-looking leader. He was only 18m 20secs ahead of Joseph Demuysere, which wasn't much in that period, and ahead of them lay a fearsome stage to Évian that featured the Lautaret, Galibier and Aravis. De Waele was not only tired by his efforts, but he was ill as well. He hardly managed to sleep the night before tackling these three passes and arrived at the start looking very pallid. Even worse, he then passed out.

Was it reasonable to allow him to start? It was because his Alcyon team had largely dominated the race. The 28-year-old Flemish rider was surrounded, protected and supported by his team-mates, even though the rules expressly forbade this. 'He ensured that we only covered 50km in three hours while he pulled himself

1929

Belgium's Maurice De Waele, who had been on the verge of abandoning even though he was wearing the yellow jersey, stuck with the race and, thanks to the support of his team, hung on to win in debatable circumstances

together,' explained Marcel Bidot. In Évian, De Waele finished with Demuysere and saved the jersey to the huge disappointment of Henri Desgrange, who fumed: 'They've allowed a corpse to win!' The following year he replaced trade teams with national teams, which marked the end of an era.

Maurice De Waele

1930

The revolution brought about by the introduction of national teams benefited the French, who had six riders in the top 10 and saw André Leducq take a splendid victory. The Tour had been reborn

André Leducq

The battle between national teams fired the enthusiasm of fans

LEDUCQ REVELS IN NEW FORMAT

Goodbye to the manufacturers! Trade teams were done away with, replaced by national line-ups whose costs (lodging, food, health care, massage) were taken care of by the race organisers, which also provided them with their bikes, which were all yellow in colour. Teams from Belgium, Italy, Spain, Germany and France lined up with so-called *touristes-routiers*, who were organised either into regional teams or rode independently.

Naturally, these reforms had to be funded and stage towns provided significant contributions. The private sector also came to the rescue, in the shape of three French companies that formed the newly created publicity caravan: they were Menier chocolate, whose publicity director Mr Thevenin had suggested the idea to Desgrange, Bayard alarm clocks and Lion shoe polish.

These companies would be grateful to the French riders, who stoked up the enthusiasm of the fans with some great performances. André Leducq finished first and Antonin Magne third, while Charles Pélissier won eight stages.

MAGNE EMERGES FROM THE SHADOWS

Antonin Magne punctured once on the Aubisque and twice on the Tourmalet, which saw Belgium's Joseph Demuysere, who was a serious candidate for the title, pass over the summit in the lead. The crucial Pau-Luchon seemed to be going all wrong for Magne, but he attacked on the descent off the Tourmalet and chased down the riders in between him and the Belgian, before rampaging on after Demuysere.

In his excitement, he had overlooked one detail: the Belgian had also suffered a puncture and was actually behind him. To defend his position, Magne had gone on the attack, which didn't exactly fit with his temperament. When he realised his mistake, he pressed on regardless and finished in Luchon 4m 42secs ahead of

1931

Antonin Magne went against his nature by attacking in the Pyrenees, then confirmed his status in the Alps before going on to succeed team-mate André Leducq as the French continued to dominate

Italy's Antonio Pesenti and 7m 44secs up on Demuysere. He also took some useful time bonuses: three minutes for a stage victory, plus three more because he had finished more than three minutes ahead of the second-placed rider. With that, Magne took the yellow jersey. He would not lose it.

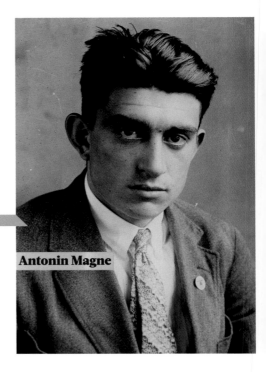

Antonin Magne

1932

Pushed all the way by an astounding performance on the part of Germany's Kurt Stöpel, André Leducq was tactically impeccable as he produced a brilliant ride to win his second Tour

André Leducq

Leducq (above) succeeded Antonin Magne (right) as France's winning run continued

LE MIROIR DES SPORTS

BONUSES BOOST LEDUCQ

The substantial time bonuses on offer at stage finishes were reconfigured: stage winners now received a four-minute time bonus, which could still be boosted by another three minutes, while the second-placed finisher earned a two-minute bonus and the third-placed rider a one-minute bonus. During the second day of the race in Nantes, this new system produced a notable first as 24-year-old Berliner Kurt Stöpel became the first German to wear the yellow jersey, having just become the first rider from his country to win a stage. He would go on to become the first German to end up on the Tour podium by finishing second in Paris.

Up to that point, the yellow jersey had been worn by riders from just five nations: France, Belgium, Italy, Luxembourg and, perhaps surprisingly, Austria, who had enjoyed that honour in 1931 thanks to *touriste-routier* Max Bulla. However, time bonuses would eventually scupper the challenge of the German champion. By Paris, Stöpel had claimed just seven minutes of bonuses, while France's André Leducq, who was always well placed and had won six stages, had clocked up 31. Willed on by the French nation, Leducq took the title by 24 minutes.

THE CLIMBING FLEA

→ In 1930, the Menier chocolate company offered 5,000 francs (approximately £3,000 nowadays) to the riders who led the race over the seven major passes on the route. Three years later, Martini-Rossi sponsored the first official Grand Prix of the Mountains. Passes were divided into different categories based on the degree of difficulty, with the riders who led over them given points that, when added up, produced the race's best climber.

Although the red polka-dot jersey didn't appear until 1975, the prestige of this award sharpened the appetite of the climbers. By leading the race over the Galibier in the Alps, the Tourmalet, Aubisque, Peyresourde, Aspin and Col de Port in the Pyrenees, and even the Ballon d'Alsace, little Vicente Trueba, dubbed 'The Flea of Torrelavega', took the mountains title. He was riding as a *touriste-routier* as there was no team from Spain, so there was no chance of Trueba troubling the rider who ended up as leader of the French team, Georges Speicher, and took the overall title.

1933

The French team's cohesion enabled 26-year-old Georges Speicher to take advantage of his position as the back-up to Antonin Magne when the 1931 champion lost all hopes of victory

Dancer and actress Josephine Baker has come to encourage the French team in Le Vésinet (opposite). Antonin Magne (below) won the Tour's first individial time-trial

1934

The sport's great rouleurs finally had the chance to show their paces with the introduction of the first individual time-trial. Antonin Magne took advantage of the opportunity to confirm his superiority

Antonin Magne

MASTER OF THE TIME-TRIAL

→ Beneath the stands of the velodrome at La-Roche-sur-Yon, which the riders had just raced into during a short road stage that morning, the 39 survivors were in the process of getting showered, replenished and massaged as they prepared for the 21st and antepenultimate stage of the race. The first rider off would be Italy's Antonio Folco, the last man in the overall standings. The other riders would follow at two-minute intervals.

For the first time the Tour was set to feature an individual time-trial, which was taking place on a 90km course between La-Roche-sur-Yon and Nantes. The innovation had been pushed by Henri Desgrange, who wanted to spice up the end of the race. Antonin Magne, who had worn the yellow jersey since the second day, was about to underline his supremacy once again by winning it (at an average speed of 35.506kmh). Italy's Giuseppe Martano, who was lying second overall, lost 8m 01secs in the test, as well as the three bonus minutes Magne claimed.

Introduced in 1934, individual time-trials have long been one of the crucial points of the Tour. Tactics don't come into play, as the best riders take the chance to create gaps on their rivals

ALL ALONE AGAINST THE CLOCK

The hierarchy of time-trial winners speaks volumes. The first four riders are: Bernard Hinault (20 victories including prologues), Eddy Merckx (16), Jacques Anquetil (11) and Miguel Indurain (10). All four riders won the Tour five times. And that's not surprising because the quality most required by this discipline is the same one that predominates when it comes to the overall classification: managing your personal capacity over a fixed distance. Jan Janssen and Greg LeMond would certainly back this up as they won the 1968 and 1989 Tours respectively on the final stage, which on both occasions was a time-trial.

Other specialists have shone, such as the American David Zabriskie, winner of the first stage in 2005 at an average speed of 54.676kmh, which remains a record for the discipline. But are such tests really comparable? What common ground is there between the 139km time-trial on the 19th stage of the 1947 Tour between Vannes and Saint-Brieuc, the 4.6km prologue at Boulogne-Billancourt in 1986 and the mountain time-trials on the Puy de Dôme (1959), the Ventoux (1987) and Alpe-d'Huez (2004)? Not a lot, apart from the solitude riders have to deal with alongside the effort and suffering.

Even that isn't a constant as time-trials are also run along team lines. Indeed, the 1927 and 1928 Tours were composed of stages of this type, but with times taken individually. They are spectacular, telegenic and provide a reminder of the very specific nature of cycling: it's an individual sport organised on team lines.

During his five victorious Tours (1991–1995), the ultra-powerful Miguel Indurain won eight of the 10 time-trials. On the occasions he did lose, he already had the Tour won

Thanks to the efforts of the entire
Saxo Bank team, Switzerland's Fabian
Cancellara is set to hang on to his yellow
jersey on the fourth stage of the 2009
Tour, a team time-trial in Montpellier

Nine times the winner of the Grand Prix des Nations
time-trial in nine appearances, Jacques Anquetil
was for many years the standard when it came to
this solo test. He is pictured on his way to victory
in 1961 between Bergerac and Périgueux

What better engine has there been than Eddy Merckx's when it comes to team time-trials? The Molteni team is heading for victory at Merlin-Plage on the third stage of the 1972 Tour, which will enable its leader to move into the yellow jersey

Bernard Hinault in 1978 between Metz and Nancy; Jean-François Bernard in 1987 on the Ventoux; Greg LeMond in 1989 on the Champs-Élysées: three different styles, but all have their eyes on the same prize – the yellow jersey

1935

Not yet 22, Belgium's Romain Maes astounded everyone by winning an incident-hit Tour in which he took the first and last stages and wore the yellow jersey from start to finish

Romain Maes

Fatigued by his efforts on the Galibier, Romain Maes recovered quickly and won on his own in Cannes

LES CYCLES ALCYON

SILLONNENT LE MONDE...

MAES WINS A DRAMA-FILLED TOUR

Romain Maes took the yellow jersey on the first stage thanks to the barrier on a level-crossing closing at an opportune moment as his rivals were pursuing him. He would keep it all the way to Paris, where he would win once again. Was he lucky? Well, there was no doubt his rivals were a lot less fortunate in what was a brutal Tour. Antonin Magne was run over during a pile-up of Tour vehicles soon after the start of the 7th stage in Aix-les-Bains when lying second overall – Belgian champion Gustave Danneels was also involved and had to abandon. Magne was able to continue but abandoned on the Col du Télégraphe, due to a wound on his right ankle that was open right to his tendon.

On the 12th stage, breakaway rider Jules Merviel received serious head injuries when he collided with a truck loaded with wood that was parked at the side of the road. On the 15th stage, the Italian Francesco Camusso, then lying third overall, collided with a vehicle and had a big crash. But the worst incident involved little Spaniard Francisco Cepeda on the descent off the Lautaret (7th stage). Having crashed and suffered a skull fracture, he was taken to hospital in Grenoble unconscious and in a critical state. He died after spending three days in a coma. Competing in the Tour for the fourth time as an individual, and a municipal judge by profession, he was just 29.

THE BATON PASSES TO GODDET

→ Now aged 71, Henri Desgrange had recently undergone surgery and his presence at the start of the race was down to bloody mindedness rather than good sense. A car had been specially prepared for him, but it only took two days for him to realise his error: he simply hadn't recovered. In Charleville, the founder and director of the Tour threw in the towel. In fact, it is more accurate to say that he passed the baton on to his spiritual son, Jacques Goddet, who had already taken over the editorship of *L'Auto* from Desgrange in 1931. The acting director, who was just 31, knew the race well – he had been following it since 1929.

As for Desgrange, he missed the extraordinary welcome that the Tour received from the first beneficiaries of the paid holidays that had been introduced by the Popular Front on 20 June. A long love story began between Sylvère Maes – whose success was founded around the victory he took on the stage between Luchon and Pau – and the yellow jersey.

1936

Maes (Sylvère) succeeded Maes (Romain), although there was no family link between them. It was indicative of the crushing domination of the Belgium team that both of them could win

Sylvère Maes (centre), the standard-bearer of the black squadron, as the Belgian national team was known

1937

Benefiting from the withdrawal of both Gino Bartali and Sylvère Maes, as well as the introduction of a new rule allowing the use of derailleurs, Roger Lapébie triumphed on his fifth attempt

Roger Lapébie

THERE'S NO DERAILING LAPÉBIE

→ Jean Leulliot, technical director of the French team, was adamant: 'The derailleur has played a major role in this Tour, and especially in Roger Lapébie's victory as he was always able to select the gear that he wanted when he wanted it.' However, the introduction of a rule allowing all riders to use a derailleur didn't have anything to do with Gino Bartali's withdrawal following a legendary crash on a descent: he fell from some way up into a mountain stream. Nor did it have anything to do with the unexpected cancellation of a team time-trial after the Belgians had totally dominated the first such test in the race. Nor, in fact, did it have anything do with the Belgians abandoning the race – even though Sylvère Maes was leading the race – in protest at the jingoistic atmosphere on the Tour. All of these factors did help Lapébie to victory, though.

Gino Bartali

BROTHERS IN ARMS

André Leducq and Antonin Magne were born in February 1904 just 12 days apart. Both riders made their Tour de France debut in 1927 and each one of them etched their name into the race's roll of honour on two occasions. 'Dédé the Ladykiller' won in 1930 and 1932, while 'Tonin the Methodical' did so in 1931 and 1934. They bid farewell to the Tour together on the 21st stage of the 1938 race between Lille and Paris. When Leducq escaped on the Côte de Vallangoujard, 55km from the finish and was quickly joined by Magne, the peloton adopted a benevolent attitude towards the pair. How could they deprive them of one final joyous moment?

In his autobiography, Leducq – for whom Magne waited even though he had a problem with his pedal – recalled: 'We had worked out exactly what we were going to do. There wouldn't be a sprint. Instead we would ride into the velodrome like brothers. Tonin then moved away, but I went up to him and put my right arm around his waist and he put his left arm around my shoulders.' They crossed the line like that, acclaimed by a crowd that was moved to tears. The peloton came home five minutes later. As a result of this action, the two riders, both giants of the sport, will appear as the joint winners of this final stage for eternity.

1938

The best climber on a Tour where he produced a series of exceptional performances, the pious Gino Bartali restored Italy's pride by taking their first overall victory since 1925

Bartali made his move towards overall victory on the stage between Digne and Briançon

1939

Belgium's Sylvère Maes added a second title to his first success in 1936. He waited until the Alps before relegating France's René Vietto into second place. But was it really all that important?

Sylvère Maes

Sylvère MAES
Belge
offert par les Bonbons
Vanluydt de Wattrelos

Nº 7

Still only 30, Sylvère Maes could well have surpassed Philippe Thys's total of three victories, but history and the war would decide otherwise

A STRANGE TOUR

There were two half-stages on the second day of the race, two more on the sixth stage, two on the eighth, a day split into three parts on stage 10, two more on stage 12, three on stage 16, two on stage 17 and two on stage 18. The race was more like a string of sausages cut up into sections than a Tour de France. In 18 days of racing there were no fewer than 28 starts and finishes. Henri Desgrange wanted the race to be cut into smaller pieces, with brief duels, in the hope that it would make for exciting racing. Instead, the action was very mediocre and the overall impression was of a huge hotchpotch.

The only real tension came from outside the race: it stemmed from the sound of boots marching to war in Europe and the rest of the world. The peloton set out without the Italians, and consequently without defending champion Gino Bartali, or the Germans, who were prevented from taking part by Mussolini and Hitler. As a result, the Belgians were invited to field two teams and there were five French regional teams. This didn't help give the event any cohesion, although the race itself was quite straightforward: René Vietto dominated until the 14th stage, but then blew apart in the Alps in the face of the battering he received from Sylvère Maes, who eased towards the title from that point on, negotiating numerous split stages as he did so.

Jean Robic

1947

The first post-war Tour produced a fantastic and totally unexpected finale when Frenchman Jean Robic claimed the title at the very last gasp without ever having worn the yellow jersey

NEVER-SAY-DIE ROBIC TRIUMPHS ON FINAL DAY

Henri Desgrange died on 16 August 1940. Jacques Goddet, who had created daily newspaper *L'Équipe* out of the ruins of *L'Auto* in 1946, fought hard to bring the Tour back to life the following year. His efforts were rewarded with an exceptional race.

At the start of the final 257km stage from Caen to Paris, the Italian Pierre Brambilla, who had taken the yellow jersey just two days before from the exhausted René Vietto, held a 53-second lead over his compatriot Aldo Ronconi, and of 2m 58secs over Jean Robic, leader of the regional West team. 'Leatherhead', 'Biquet', 'Death-dodger' – there was no lack of nicknames for this 26-year-old Breton who had actually been born in the Ardennes.

His bluntness was as legendary as his tenacity. On the way out of Rouen, with 135km to the finish, Robic attacked on the Côte de Bonsecours. He was quickly joined by Édouard Fachleitner from the France team, who was lying fifth overall at 6m 55secs, and left Brambilla and Ronconi to their fate as he committed himself to his task despite repeated attacks from his breakaway companion.

'You won't be able to win,' he told Fachleitner. 'Let's cooperate and I will give you 100,000 francs!' In Paris, Jean Robic won the Tour de France without having ever worn the yellow jersey, finishing 3m 58secs up on Fachleitner. Poor Brambilla finished third at 10m 07secs.

Majestic on the Izoard, Jean Robic gradually chipped away to make up for earlier losses. He was the only one who believed he had a chance of winning

BARTALI WINS A DECADE ON

He had been 24 in 1938 when he won the Tour de France for the first time. Being 10 years older didn't stop him from repeating that success. Philippe Thys achieved the same feat, adding a victory in 1920 after the Great War to his previous two in 1913 and 1914. But there was less of a gap between the Belgian's successes.

History outside the race was about to have an impact on history within it. In Cannes, at the end of the 12th stage, Bartali was lying only seventh overall, 21m 28secs behind Frenchman Louison Bobet, and that despite flying away from his rivals in the Pyrenees. At his hotel that evening, Bartali received a call from Italian prime minister Alcide De Gasperi, who told him that communist leader Palmiro Togliatti had just been shot three times in an assassination attempt. The country was on the edge of chaos. 'We need you,' the prime minister told Bartali, who replied, 'What can I do? I am at the Tour.' De Gasperi told him, 'You can do a lot by winning stages...'

Subsequently, Gino the patriot went on to win the 13th stage in Briançon, the 14th in Aix-les-Bains, where he also took the yellow jersey, and the 15th in Lausanne. He claimed a final success in Liège and won the Tour with an advantage of 26m 16secs over Brik Schotte and 28m 48secs over Guy Lapébie. It was quite some response!

1948

Italy's Gino Bartali repeated the success he'd taken way back in 1938, without offering the least opportunity to his rivals, among whom was the young and impressive Louison Bobet

Gino Bartali attacked 20km from the summit of the Croix-de-Fer. Only Louison Bobet and André Brulé managed to stay with him

Gino Bartali

ENTENTE CORDIALE

The great Gino Bartali devoted himself to helping his younger compatriot Fausto Coppi (left), and led him towards his first Tour de France success

His CV already featured three victories in Milan-San Remo, four in the Tour of Lombardy and, most notably, three in the Giro d'Italia, the most recent of which had been claimed just a few weeks earlier. It was no wonder that much was expected of Fausto Coppi as he made his Tour debut aged almost 30, especially as he was in the same Italian team as Gino Bartali, who was defending the title. Was cohabitation possible between them?

Things started badly. On the fifth stage between Rouen and Saint-Malo, Jacques Marinelli and Coppi were struggling to hang on after the feed station at Caen. They fell. The Italian suffered a broken wheel and forks and had to be given a new bike. He was clearly unhappy and waited for his directeur sportif.

His morale in the gutter, he finished the stage 19 minutes down. It seemed his chance had gone and he talked about abandoning.

He kept going thanks to Bartali's encouragement. He won the time-trial, looked his old self in the Pyrenees and attacked in the Alps. Between Cannes and Briançon, the two Italians took off: 'Let's attack together,' Bartali suggested. 'It's my 35th birthday today. Tomorrow you will win the Tour.' Finally, there was an *entente cordiale*. Bartali wore the yellow jersey for a day and ceded it to Coppi at Aosta. The 'Campionissimo', who took the title in Paris ahead of Bartali, became the first man to complete the Giro-Tour double – not a bad achievement for a rider who had looked completely out of the running.

1949

Making his debut in the Tour de France, Italy's Fausto Coppi took the title thanks to the help he got from team-mate Gino Bartali, despite being his main rival

Fausto Coppi

1950

Ferdinand Kübler took hold of the yellow jersey that the Italians gave up when they abandoned the race, and took advantage to provide Switzerland with its first success

Ferdinand Kübler

THE ITALIANS RETREAT

→ Gino Bartali won the 11th stage between Pau and Saint-Gaudens, and on that same day the yellow jersey ended up on the shoulders of Fiorenzo Magni. Everything was going the way of the Italians – or at least it seemed that way until they all decided to abandon the race an hour before the start of the following stage as a result of the actions of a few spectators on the Col d'Aspin. A press motorbike had swerved on the climb, causing Bartali, Bobet and Robic to collide with each other. Some French fans blamed the Italian for the resulting crash. Bartali played the martyr, saying that a man had rushed towards him with a knife in his hand. 'I've been the victim of assault and battery, which has no place in honest sporting activity. I am not going to continue,' said Bartali.

His directeur sportif, Alfredo Binda, sided with him but allowed the other Italians the option of continuing. 'I am crying because I can't accept the yellow jersey,' Magni declared. 'I was selected with a view to helping Bartali and not with the goal of winning the Tour de France. I can't stay when Bartali has retired.'

All of the Italians responded in the same way, which gave rise to a rumour that Bartali had used this pretext to avoid being beaten by Magni, his compatriot and rival.

Ferdi Kübler inherited the yellow jersey and held it all the way to Paris.

Hugo Koblet

1951

A first Swiss success was followed by another: Hugo Koblet not only won the race with a great show of strength, but also earned a very gentlemanly nickname – 'The Pedaller of Charm'

HUGO SHOWS HIS CLASS

→ The short stage (177km) between Brive and Agen shouldn't have upset the overall standings. When the French rider Deprez, who had attacked after 35km with Castellin, found himself alone at the front it hardly seemed like news at all. However, when he was joined and then dropped by Hugo Koblet, a demonstration of power began. The Swiss had 135km ahead of him and was only 1m 15secs up on the peloton. Yes, Bobet did puncture and for a while the French team dragged its heels. But then Coppi, Magni, Geminiani, Bartali, Bobet, Ockers, Robic and the others cooperated for 70km. But it was in vain. Koblet won the stage – at an average of 39kmh – ahead of a furious group of chasers who were far from happy to see that they had lost 2m 35secs. With his leather gloves, watch on his wrist, his goggles perched on his forehead or around his left arm, and a little sponge in his pocket with which to wipe his brow, the Swiss was elegance personified.

TELEVISION TUNES IN

→ His name was Henri Persin and he was making his debut in the peloton at the Tour de France. He featured in plenty of breakaways, although he never turned a pedal in anger. A pillion passenger on a motorbike, this broadcast cameraman was the first to record 16mm images for RTF, French national television. At stage finishes, his films were dispatched to Paris, where they were developed and edited before Georges de Caunes added the commentary that accompanied them when they were broadcast. Thanks to this initiative on the part of Pierre Sabbagh, the Tour de France, as well as its victor Fausto Coppi, was beamed into French homes, or at least into the 30,000 that possessed a receiver.

This was only the start. Sixty years on, more than 120 television networks are present on the Tour. The media corps in general (including the written press, radio and television) is 4,000-strong: there are 2,400 journalists, photographers and TV commentators, plus 1,600 technicians and drivers.

1952

With Bobet, Kübler and Koblet absent, Fausto Coppi crushed the opposition and finished more than 28 minutes ahead of the runner-up to claim his second success after his win in 1949

At Nancy (stage 7), Alpe-d'Huez (10), Sestrières (11), Pau (18) and on the Puy de Dôme (21), Fausto Coppi was first over the line. He was quite simply peerless

Fausto Coppi

The green jersey was intended to raise the profile of the sprinters, but it was all-rounder Fritz Schaer who claimed the first points title

1953

On this sixth Tour appearance, Louison Bobet finally added sporting glory to his immense popularity as the Swiss Fritz Schaer claimed the first green jersey

Louison Bobet

VICTORY ON POINTS

Between 1905 and 1912, the Tour's overall title was decided on points, which were allocated depending on each rider's finishing position at stage finishes, with an extra point added to a rider's total if he finished more than five minutes behind the man ahead. Subsequently, and more logically, the winner was once again the rider who took the least amount of time to cover the route.

In 1953, to celebrate the 50th anniversary of the race, the organisers decided to establish a new competition that would reward the most consistent rider at stage finishes. The idea was to give the sprinters a chance to shine, as they were too limited in the mountains to be able to contend for the overall title. Green was chosen as the colour of the new jersey worn by the leader of this classification simply because the company sponsoring it made lawnmowers.

Switzerland's Fritz Schaer, 27, quickly got to grips with the new competition: he won the first stage in Metz, then the second in Liège. He then finished fourth in Pau, Cotterêts and Luchon (in the mountains), fifth in Monaco, seventh in Briançon and third in the Saint-Étienne time-trial. He ended up sixth overall, 18m 44secs down on Louison Bobet and only 3m 42secs away from the podium.

The creation of the green jersey enabled a hierarchy to be established between the sprinters, who are half-rider, half-acrobat. Their domain lies within the final straight

SPEED DEMONS

For the most part sprinters remain in the background. When the road climbs, they disappear from view, trailing along in the *gruppetto*, the often large group of dropped riders who ride in front of the broom wagon with the sole objective of finishing within the time limit. Some of them even disappear completely, like Mario Cipollini. The Italian rode eight Tours de France between 1992 and 2004 and never saw Paris. In fact, he never went further than the 11th stage. His plan was always to abandon. Even when the road is flat, the sprinters aren't very apparent, or at least they aren't until the final few hundred metres. Up to that point, they hide, take shelter, seek protection. In other words, they preserve their resources for as long as possible. Then they move into the wheels of their team-mates, who have the responsibility for setting them up for victory. These riders are the equivalent of football's midfielders, the players who provide the decisive pass. The sprinters are the centre forwards who run on to it.

Among the archetypal sprinters are Freddy Maertens, the Belgian who won eight stages in the 1976 Tour to establish himself as the successor to Frenchman Charles Pélissier, who pulled off the same feat in 1930. Others are André Darrigade, who took 22 stage wins between 1953 and 1964, and Mark Cavendish, who has claimed 23 between 2008 and 2012. Erik Zabel only won 12 stages over 14 Tours, but the German, who was less explosive and powerful than these riders, was more consistent and complete, and his speciality was the green jersey. He won it six years in a row between 1996 and 2001, and knew that points meant prizes.

With their over-developed thighs and gritted teeth, the 21st-century sprinters look as if they have come from a Japanese manga comic. The sprinter heading the charge on this occasion is Mark Cavendish, who is leading Norwegian Thor Hushovd in his green jersey

Belgium's Freddy Maertens won eight stages in 1976, equalling the record that Charles Pélissier set in 1930. He won seven more in 1978 and 1981. He rode just three Tours, taking the green jersey on each occasion, and taking the secret to his success with him

Rik Van Looy claimed four stages and the green
jersey in 1963. The pick of them came in the
Parc des Princes. The Belgian looks radiant and
permits himself a smile as he crosses the line
as there is no other rider who can match him

A six-day racing specialist, Rik Van Steenbergen felt particularly at home on the track. On this occasion, in 1949, the Parc des Princes provides him with one of his 23 stage wins in the grand tours. He was also crowned world champion on three occasions

Between 1953 and 1964, France's André Darrigade steadily built up an impressive collection of stage wins (22 in total), and specialised in taking the first of the race, a feat he achieved on no less than five occasions: in 1956-1959 and 1961

Laurent Jalabert (top) at Armentières in 1994, and Djamolidin Abdoujaparov (bottom right) on the Champs-Élysées in 1991 paid a high price for their risk-taking. André Darrigade (bottom left, wrapped in bandages) is hugged by Charly Gaul in the Parc des Princes in 1958

Germany's Erik Zabel, Britain's Mark Cavendish, Belgium's Tom Boonen and Italy's Alessandro Petacchi (clockwise from top left): four major stars from the 1990s and 2000s who are united by the same gesture – that of victory

Mario Cipollini in his pomp. Over eight
Tours between 1992 and 2004, the
Italian won 12 bunch sprints, but never
finished the race. As soon as the road
went up, he used to abandon

Four stage victories in 2008, six in 2009, five in 2010 and 2011, and three in 2012... Mark Cavendish affirms: 'I'm an old-style sprinter. I'm incapable of climbing a mountain, but if I'm in front 200m from the line, no one can beat me.' Tyler Farrar and Alessandro Petacchi bear witness to that.

Louison Bobet

TOUR DE FRANCE 54
Le Parisien libéré
853
L'ÉQUIPE
1e ET 9e Étapes

1954

Having finished the race in exceptional fashion with victories at Briançon and in the Epinal-Nancy time-trial, Louison Bobet retained his title ahead of Switzerland's Ferdi Kübler

Majestic on the Izoard, the climb he made his own, Louison Bobet opened such a gap on his pursuers that the final stages were only a formality. His second yellow jersey created jubilation across France

HOLLAND HOSTS THE FIRST FOREIGN START

→ Since the first time the Tour went beyond France's borders, when it crossed into Germany in 1906, six other countries had welcomed the race onto their soil: Switzerland (for the first time in 1907), Monaco (1939), Belgium (1947), Luxembourg (1947), Italy (1948) and Spain (1949). But on this occasion the Tour headed to a country with which France did not share a border. In addition, the Grand Départ took place there on 8 July.

What was the reason for this innovation? It was feared that the first Tour of Europe, which had been organised by the weekly *Route et Piste* and was due to the take place in September, might overshadow the Tour de France. This new race would start in Paris and finish in Strasbourg after having passed

through Belgium, Luxembourg, Germany, Austria, Italy and Switzerland.

Jacques Goddet reacted quickly. He chose the Netherlands – which was not on the itinerary of the Tour d'Europe – to launch his counter-attack. It was also no coincidence that Amsterdam was willing to pay a very high price for this honour.

No one would regret it. The welcome the race got was exceptional and the sense of occasion incredible as the Dutch danced to the sound of Yvette Horner's accordion. The icing on the cake was the fact that one of their own, Wout Wagtmans, won the stage between Amsterdam and Brasschaat (Belgium) and took the yellow jersey. Ferdi Kübler had already lost nine minutes to Bobet – and wouldn't get it back.

TOUR DE FRANCE-NUMMER *Sport* EN SPORTWERELD
DE GELE TRUI
1954
VAN WESTERTOREN TOT EIFFELTOREN
PRIJS 50 CENTS

1955

Louison Bobet wrapped up a third victory in succession, putting himself alongside Philippe Thys as the only three-time winners of the race. The Breton suffered throughout with an injury in a very delicate place...

THE MOUNTAIN THAT SPOKE VOLUMES

→ The Ventoux is known as 'The Bald Mountain'. It may be bald, but it isn't mute. When the riders tackled it during the 11th stage between Marseille and Avignon, the mountain spoke volumes about practices related to doping, most notably as a result of the serious difficulties that affected Jean Malléjac. The French rider started to totter, then collapsed and fell unconscious. His jaws had to be forced apart to make him drink, and then he had to have an injection and be given oxygen to bring him back to consciousness. The meandering and delirium of Ferdi Kübler on the same road for the same reasons – after pausing at one point, he set off again in the wrong direction – were, thankfully, nothing more than an anecdote, as was the mysterious 'stomach upset' that hit Charly Gaul. It was all very worrying.

The Ventoux also said a great deal about those who were on form. Malléjac and Kübler were eliminated, Gaul lost six minutes, Ockers 17, and Bauvin 32. That was the end of their hopes. Only the Belgian Jean Brankart resisted. He would finish second in Paris because the Ventoux never lies. The stage's solo winner, Louison Bobet, wearing his world champion's jersey before exchanging it for the yellow jersey, would end up taking his third victory in succession. The pain caused by a wound on his buttock – undoubtedly a saddle sore – forced him to stand on the pedals a good deal of the time, but it didn't stop him.

Louison Bobet

Wearing his world champion's jersey, Bobet produced a huge performance on the slopes of the Ventoux

Roger Walkowiak

A BITTERSWEET SUCCESS

Of the 31 riders in the break who finished 18m 46secs up on the seemingly unconcerned peloton on the Lorient-Angers stage, only one would be able to resist the eventual pursuers, who finally started to live up to their billing as Tour favourites. Roger Walkowiak, 29 and a good rider, finished 19th in Angers and surprised everyone by holding off the climbers – notably Charly Gaul and Federico Bahamontes – in the mountains, while also limiting his losses in the time-trials. In Paris, he still held a lead of 1m 25secs over Gilbert Bauvin, who had been unlucky in the Pyrenees, where he fell. Jacques Goddet invented the phrase 'to win à la Walkowiak', but for a lot of observers the phrase took on a negative connotation.

They were particularly critical of the victor because he hadn't won a single stage. That would result in the image developing of Walkowiak being a usurper, even though he had won the Tour on the road. In 1960, at the end of his career, he cut all ties with cycling and returned to working in a factory after having run a bar, where the constant questions from his customers about the value of his victory used to wear him down.

1956

A surprise breakaway offered Roger Walkowiak from the North-East/ Centre team the chance of his life. He seized it and became one of the Tour's most astonishing winners

André Darrigade swapped his French national champion's jersey for yellow at the end of the first stage. But it was the 'usurper' Roger Walkowiak who carried the yellow jersey into Paris

Jacques Anquetil

1957

Young Tour debutant Jacques Anquetil built up a lead then closed the door on his rivals, helped by an extremely powerful French team, to claim a win that showed maturity beyond his years

ANQUETIL REIGNS SUPREME

→ France won the team prize, claiming 13 stage victories and monopolising the yellow jersey for the whole of the Tour, except for a brief fling on the part of regional rider Nicolas Barone on the eighth stage. André Darrigade (three stage wins), René Privat (three), Jean Stablinski (one) and green jersey winner Jean Forestier provided marvellous support to a 23-year-old Tour debutant from Normandy. Jacques Anquetil, unbeatable in the time-trials on the Montjuich (Spain) and in Libourne, also won the road stage into his home city of Rouen, as well as the stage into Thonon-les-Bains. He wore the yellow jersey for 16 days and the Parc des Princes celebrated the coronation of a new king.

1958

Tour de France? It was more like the Tour de Gaul as the Luxembourger claimed victory having taken the yellow jersey thanks to his success in the time-trial on the penultimate day. What followed was tragic

Charly Gaul

TRAGEDY STRIKES AGAIN

→ In 1957, the radio journalist Alex Virot and his motorbike driver René Wagner were killed when they crashed into a ravine during the Barcelona to Ax-les-Thermes stage. On this occasion, a similar drama unfolded in the Parc des Princes right in front of the eyes of the watching spectators. André Darrigade seemed to be on the verge of winning his sixth stage in the race. Coming into the final 200m, he had just gone a few lengths clear of Italy's Pierino Baffi and Frenchman Jean Graczyk, who was in the green jersey, when he collided with the secretary-general of the Parc, who had wandered onto the edge of the track. The sprinter came away with just five stitches in his forehead and a blistering headache. Constant Wouters, on the other hand, was much more severely injured. He died 11 days later.

FRENCH FIGHT AMONG THEMSELVES

→ Brilliantly cohesive in 1957, the French national team's hopes were sunk by disunity just two years later. At the start, it looked like a dream team, with Jacques Anquetil, Louison Bobet, Raphaël Geminiani and Roger Rivière, especially as all four had signed a collaboration pact. By the finish, Bobet had abandoned, Geminiani was 28th overall at 1h 44mins, Rivière was fourth at 5m 17secs and Anquetil third at 5m 05secs.

By watching each other, the latter pair played into the hands of Spain's Federico Bahamontes, 31, who ended up winning just a short time-trial on the Puy-de-Dôme, as well as Frenchman Henry Anglade (from the Centre-Midi team), who won in Aurillac. These two riders, described as 'free men' in *L'Équipe*, finished first and second, respectively, in a race beset by foolishness. The fans showed their disgust when the French team arrived in Paris. The fans booed Anquetil and jeered Rivière. Only green jersey winner André Darrigade was spared.

Federico Bahamontes

1959

Climber Federico Bahamontes became the first Spanish winner of the Tour de France. The French national team, riven by internal rivalries, proved to be a big help

Federico Bahamontes (left) imposes his rhythm, but Roger Rivière sticks with him

1960

The winner in Paris, Italy's Gastone Nencini, dedicated his victory bouquet to his unfortunate rival Roger Rivière, who was left disabled for life after crashing on a descent

FAMILLE DES GRANDS CHAMPIONS ITALIENS

Gastone Nencini

2. NENCINI

Photo MIROIR-SPRINT

Roger Rivière's career is over after a terrible crash

RIVIÈRE'S TERRIBLE CRASH

→ At the start of the 14th stage from Millau to Avignon, 24-year-old Frenchman Roger Rivière was lying second overall, 1m 38secs behind Italian Gastone Nencini, who had been placed in a potentially winning position when Rivière had scuppered the hopes of his team-mate Henry Anglade on the road to Lorient. The leader was a good rouleur and climber, but he was best known as a fabulous descender. When he attacked on the descent of the Perjuret in the Cévennes, Rivière made the mistake of trying to follow him. It wasn't long before the Frenchman left the road, went over the parapet and landed 20 metres below.

By a miracle, he survived, but his career ended there. Victim of a double fracture of the spinal column, he ended up 80 per cent disabled. During three-and-a-half years as a professional, he had won three world pursuit titles and set two world hour records, the second of which (47.346km) stood until 1967.

A second yellow jersey for Jacques Anquetil after his success in 1957, and a second green jersey for André Darrigade after his victory in 1959. The two French champions shone brightly in Paris

Jacques Anquetil

1961

Never attacked nor even threatened, Jacques Anquetil claimed the title again four years on from his first success. He wore the yellow jersey from the first evening to the last

ANQUETIL'S MERRY DANCE

André Darrigade won the first half-stage between Rouen and Versailles, but lost the lead on the second, a 28km time-trial at Versailles, where his brief hold on the yellow jersey was ended by Jacques Anquetil. That was the first and final change at the top of the overall standings. Anquetil never lost his grip on the lead from there on.

The French team, which carried off the team classification and the green jersey thanks to Darrigade, totally controlled the race and no one was able to trouble them, much to the dismay of Jacques Goddet, who dubbed the other riders 'the dwarves of the road'. He described them as powerless, cowardly, resigned to their fate and satisfied with their own mediocrity.

Satisfied with their own mediocrity? On the final stage between Tours and Paris, Italy's Guido Carlesi managed to beat Luxembourg's Charly Gaul by six seconds and nudge him out of second place overall by just two miserable seconds! Anquetil won as he wanted and beat his fellow podium finishers by more than 12 minutes.

THE RETURN OF TRADE TEAMS

→ It needed six years of negotiations for the organisers, who were very attached to the formula of national teams, to accept a return to the trade team formula that allowed sponsors to benefit from being in the shop window that the Tour had become. Consequently, Jacques Anquetil was no longer wearing the blue, white and red of France, but the jersey of ACCB-Saint Raphaël-Helyett-Hutchinson. Anquetil remained faithful to his own image of being sure in his own ability and equally certain of the weakness of others. He seemed to calculate precisely so that he didn't take the yellow jersey until the end of the stage 20 time-trial. He scooped the title once again, finishing five minutes up on Belgian Joseph Planckaert.

Within the Mercier-BP-Hutchinson team, another Frenchman established the foundations of what was to be his reputation in the years to come: unlucky, courageous and popular. He started the race with his wrist in plaster, lost eight minutes right away, won in Aix-les-Bains and finished on the podium 10 minutes behind Anquetil. Raymond Poulidor had arrived.

Jacques Anquetil

1962

A third success for the metronome-like Jacques Anquetil, who was happy enough to take advantage of his time-trialling superiority to ensure his supremacy

1963

Jacques Anquetil won the 50th Tour, finishing ahead of Federico Bahamontes in a very mountainous race

Jacques Anquetil

ANQUETIL RULES IN THE MOUNTAINS

→ On a course that the organisers had intended would not suit the defending champion because it had fewer time-trials and more mountains, Jacques Anquetil got the better of the climbers on their own terrain. He won at Bagnères-de-Bigorre and even took the yellow jersey from the Spaniard Federico Bahamontes in Chamonix at the end of the 17th stage. As he was also still winning the time-trials, he had no trouble taking the title again.

The reception he got from the fans in Paris was completely the opposite to that reserved for Raymond Poulidor, who was whistled, booed and accused of being passive – the French public had expecting him to attack – colluding with Anquetil and even riding against Bahamontes on occasions. However, Poulidor, who ended up 17 minutes down in eighth place, was undoubtedly lacking form.

1964

At the end of a fantastic duel with the ideal runner-up, Jacques Anquetil was crowned the Tour de France's first five-time winner after beating Raymond Poulidor by just 55 seconds

The battle between Anquetil and Poulidor on the slopes of the Puy de Dôme remains one of the greatest moments in Tour history. The two men remained almost inseparable all the way into Paris

Jacques Anquetil

A FIVE-STAR TOUR

Coming out of the Alps in Monaco at the end of the ninth stage, Raymond Poulidor was lying third overall, 15 seconds ahead of Jacques Anquetil in fifth. Arriving in Pau after the Pyrenees, the gap was even narrower: just nine seconds, but now Anquetil was in third ahead of Poulidor in fourth. The two men couldn't be separated. Although victory in the time-trial the next day put Anquetil into the yellow jersey, his advantage over Poulidor was only 56 seconds as they prepared to take on the Puy de Dôme, two days before the finish.

Their battle there has taken on legendary status. Wheel to wheel, shoulder to shoulder, they climbed side by side for a dozen kilometres in front of half a million fans. Anquetil resisted and managed to hide his suffering. He was bluffing, but Poulidor fell for it and didn't dare attack. When he finally made a move a kilometre from the summit, Anquetil yielded metre after metre, but hung on. He only lost 42 seconds.

Anquetil, sticken with fatigue, had saved the yellow jersey by 14 seconds, but he knew that he would extend that advantage in the final time-trial between Versailles and Paris. In the end he pushed his lead out to 55 seconds to seal his fifth victory (after those in 1957 and 1961-1963) and achieve the Giro-Tour double that only Coppi had previously achieved in 1949 and 1952. His victory was doubly historic.

PHOTO STORY

In winning the 1964
Tour de France, Jacques
Anquetil founded a
very elite club: that of the
five-time Tour winners

THE FIVE-TIME CLUB

→ In 1908, Lucien Petit-Breton introduced a new type of rider to the Tour: those who had won more than one title. Maurice Garin had held that honour, but was disqualified for cheating after his second victory in 1904. Next came the three-time winners, a group inaugurated by Philippe Thys. The Belgian would surely have done even better if the Great War hadn't deprived him of further opportunities. He took the title in 1913 and 1914, and then again in 1920. Louison Bobet joined him after taking three wins on the trot in 1953, 1954 and 1955. Greg LeMond joined this duo much later (1986, 1989, 1990).

Other riders have achieved even greater success – a lot greater in fact. Five giants of the race crushed all the marks that had been established before them. Initially there was Jacques Anquetil, who won five Tours (1957, 1961-1964), wore the yellow jersey on 52 occasions and took 16 stage wins. Then came 'The Cannibal'. Eddy Merckx also won five (1969-1972, 1974), wore the yellow jersey 111 times and bagged 34 stage wins, marks that still stand as records. Then came Bernard Hinault (1978, 1979, 1981, 1982 and 1985), 79 yellow jerseys and 28 stage wins, and Miguel Indurain (1991-1995), with 60 yellow jerseys and 12 stage wins.

Lance Armstrong surpassed his predecessors, winning seven in a row between 1999 and 2005 (81 yellow jerseys, 22 stage victories), before his victories were struck from the record books in 2012. But even before his cheating was exposed, he never generated the same kind of enthusiasm or admiration as his predecessors. That was a sign of the times. In the 21st century it became hard to believe in miracles.

Disgraced Lance Armstrong always employed the same tactic: destroy the hopes of his rivals on the first mountain stage, knowing that they would never be able to better him in the time-trials

Philippe Thys lost 6kg during the 1920 race. But he still won his third Tour title after those of 1913 and 1914. What would his record have been like without the Great War?

Louison Bobet had to wait until his sixth
Tour de France before finally taking the title
in 1953. But he then added successive wins
in 1954 (when he is seen being congratulated
by accordionist Yvette Horner) and 1955

In spite of Raymond Poulidor's resistance, most notably on the Puy de Dôme (top), Jacques Anquetil won his fourth title in a row in 1964. It was the fifth and last of his extraordinary career

In 1957, the young Jacques Anquetil is congratulated by his manager Daniel Dousset after his first Tour success, which came on his first appearance in the race. He was only 23 years old

Raymond Poulidor, Felice Gimondi and Joop Zoetemelk (from left to right) surround race leader Eddy Merckx. One of the Belgian's best qualities was that he beat such great rivals

In 1970, en route towards his second success, Merckx is on the attack with the young Lucien Van Impe, who would have to wait until the end of The Cannibal's career before winning the Tour in 1976

1978, 1979, 1981, 1982... Neither Joop Zoetemelk nor Robert Alban (above) can prevent Bernard Hinault winning again. But he would have to wait until 1985 before taking his fifth victory

Fierce determination, power, talent,
tactical sense and even panache...
Bernard Hinault had it all. He was the last
of the great winners for whom the Tour
was not the sole objective of the season

Unbeatable in time-trials, Miguel Indurain also showed off his power in the mountains. Luc Leblanc and Richard Virenque could only follow him. The Spaniard won five times in succession

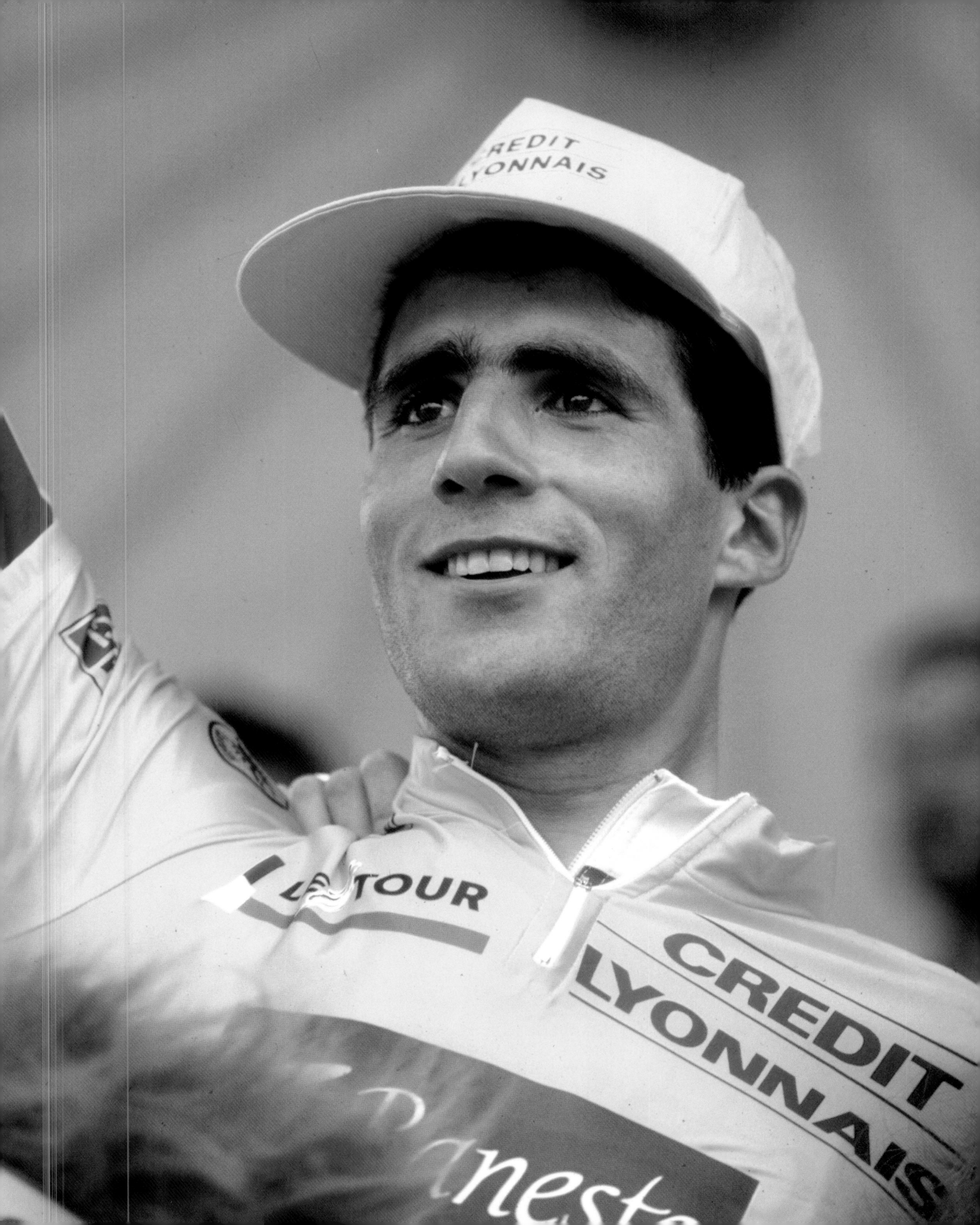
CREDIT
LYONNAIS
TOUR
CREDIT
LYONNAIS

1965

Called up as a late replacement for the Tour by his team after finishing third in the Giro, young Felice Gimondi, 23, not only started his first Tour but won it, beating Raymond Poulidor

Raymond Poulidor sets a pace that Julio Jiménez is struggling to follow... The Frenchman would end up beating the Spanish climber on his preferred terrain

POULIDOR'S EXPLOITS IN VAIN

→ Julio Jiménez was dazzling as he steadily moved towards victory in the mountains competition. The Spaniard had no ambitions for the overall classification, but took prestigious wins when the road went upwards. The one stage he really wanted to win was 14, which finished on the summit of Mont Ventoux.

Raymond Poulidor needed to distance his rivals and, at the same time, cut his deficit on Felice Gimondi, who was wearing the yellow jersey. Incredibly, the Frenchman followed the rhythm set by the Spaniard and managed to stay on terms with him. A few hundred metres from the summit, Jiménez punctured and Poulidor won the stage, finishing six seconds ahead of the King of the Mountains. However, Poulidor's exploits didn't turn out the way he had hoped. Tour debutant Gimondi had hung on doggedly behind and lost only 1m 38secs to the Frenchman, saving his yellow jersey by 35 seconds. He would extend that advantage in the last two time-trials, reaching Paris with a lead of 2m 40secs over Poulidor.

ANQUETIL PLAYS HIS JOKER

→ There was open warfare between Jacques Anquetil and Raymond Poulidor, who were no longer on speaking terms. So when Lucien Aimar found himself in a breakaway on the 10th stage between Bayonne and Pau, Anquetil laughed quietly to himself. He lost seven minutes that day and without doubt his hopes of winning the Tour. But Poulidor, who had been marking him tightly, lost just as much. They were wrapped up in a game of 'If I lose, you lose'. But the five-time winner held a joker in the shape of Aimar, who was one of his Ford team-mates. From that point on, Anquetil did all he could to protect Aimar and he gave him a definite nudge in the right direction when he marked Poulidor after his Ford team-mate had broken away on the descent of the Col de Braida during the 17th stage from Briançon to Turin, where Aimar gained 2m 02secs on Anquetil's great rival. At the finish in Paris, the gap between Aimar and third-placed Raymond Poulidor was 2m 02secs...

Team-mates at Ford, Lucien Aimar (left) and Jacques Anquetil seem happy to have tricked their rivals

Lucien Aimar

1966

Struck by illness, Jacques Anquetil pulled out of what turned out to be his final Tour. But he had enough time before that to set up victory for one of his lieutenants, Lucien Aimar

Roger Pingeon

1967

At the age of 27, France's Roger Pingeon was crowned champion at the end of a Tour marked by the death of Britain's Tom Simpson on the slopes of Mont Ventoux

PINGEON CATCHES HIS RIVALS OFF GUARD

It was only a half-stage, but it ended up counting as much as any full stage. The 172km between Roubaix and Jambes (in Belgium) on the fifth day of the race made all the difference. A group went clear after about 50km. It contained several outsiders plus Roger Pingeon, who was third in the hierarchy of the France team behind Raymond Poulidor and Lucien Aimar – national teams had returned for this year's Tour.

The opportunity was too good to miss. Pingeon tested his rivals on the Mur de Thuin, then took off in Marcinelle. He had 57km left to cover on his own, and the riders behind split into two groups that came in 1m 24secs and 2m 27secs behind him. More importantly, the peloton containing the big favourites rolled in 6m 22secs down. That handed him the yellow jersey and led to a reshaping of priorities in the French team.

Raymond Poulidor demonstrated admirable self-sacrifice by protecting Pingeon in the Alps. Poulidor had plenty of reason to be down. He had missed out on the yellow jersey in the Tour's first-ever prologue, finishing just six seconds behind unexpected winner José Maria Errandonea. Then he suffered an inexplicably bad day on the Ballon d'Alsace, which meant that his own Tour hopes were over on the eighth stage. It was Pingeon's time that had come.

Jan Janssen was Dutch and wore glasses. Statistically, these two characteristics tended to count against a rider winning the Tour, but he managed to upset the odds

Jan Janssen

1968

Jan Janssen became the first Dutch winner of the Tour thanks to his victory in the final time-trial, which left him just 38 seconds ahead of Herman Van Springel

REVOLUTION AT THE TOUR

→ At the start of the second half of the split stage on the final day, Belgium's Herman Van Springel was in the yellow jersey and had a lead of 12 seconds on Spain's Gregorio San Miguel, 16 on Dutchman Jan Janssen and 58 on Italy's Franco Bitossi. There were four men within a minute of each other and nine within two-and-a-half! The race would be decided in a 55.2km time-trial between Melun and Paris.

Halfway through, the verdict was almost sealed: only Van Springel and Janssen were still in the hunt. Even better for the Belgian, rather than losing time he had gained two seconds on the Dutchman. However, riding a lighter bike and apparently better informed by his directeur sportif, Janssen began to up his pace. He gained second after second and finished flat out in a time 54 seconds quicker than the Belgian's.

Van Springel was inconsolable, and to this day still casts doubt on the speed of the bespectacled Dutchman that day. Janssen, 28, pulled on the yellow jersey that he hadn't previously worn during the race to give the Netherlands its first Tour de France title, achieved with the smallest winning margin registered up to that point. 1968 really was a year of revolution.

Eddy Merckx

THE CANNIBAL EMERGES

At the finish in Paris, Eddy Merckx won the Tour de France with an advantage of almost 18 minutes on the runner-up, having spent 20 days in the yellow jersey. He won the points competition, the mountains classification, the combined jersey and helped Faema to win the team prize. He won the stages into Belfort, Divonne-les-Bains, Digne, Revel, Mourenx and, of course, Paris to round off his triumphal procession. He also claimed the prize as the most aggressive rider because, even in the absence of a rival of his stature, the young man kept on fighting – against himself.

On the 17th stage from Luchon to Mourenx, Merckx sprinted to the summit of the Tourmalet to make sure he led the race over the top. A small gap opened of just a few seconds and the Belgian took full advantage. All alone, he continued with his effort. At Argelès, he was 1m 30secs ahead. At the foot of the Soulor his lead was 3m 30secs. At the summit it was 4m 55secs. He kept on going. He was seven minutes clear going over the Aubisque and extended his lead to eight minutes over his nearest pursuers by the finish in Mourenx. Former winners Gimondi and Janssen came in quarter of an hour behind.

Why did he do it? On the morning of his fantastic ride, he was 8m 21secs ahead of Pingeon and 9m 29secs up on Gimondi in the overall standings. He did it because he could.

1969

Twenty-four-year-old Eddy Merckx discovered all about the Tour and its numerous classifications. Not a single one of them escaped his voracious appetite. The Belgian wanted to win it all – and win with panache

On his first appearance at the Tour, Belgium's Eddy Merckx scooped all the classifications and all the jerseys and even put on a free show in the mountains

1970

Eddy Merckx bagged eight stage victories and the title of best climber as well as completing the Giro-Tour double. It was hard to imagine anyone troubling him

Young Bernard Thévenet, 22, makes a name for himself in the midst of the Eddy Merckx show by winning at La Mongie on 14 July

Eddy Merckx

THÉVENET LIGHTS UP BASTILLE DAY

→ Bernard Thévenet was only 22 years old and owed his participation in the Tour de France to the last-minute withdrawals of Ferdinand Bracke and Gerben Karstens from the Peugeot team. It has to be said that, until the 18th stage, Thévenet gone through the race without attracting a great deal of attention, apart from when he had finished fifth on the Ventoux. But, after passing over the Cols de Menté, Peyresourde and Aspin, when the small leading group started up the climb to La Mongie on the slopes of the Tourmalet, the debutant felt good. Merckx, Zoetemelk, Pettersson and Van Impe were there, but it was Thévenet who attacked 8km from the finish and went off after Gilbert Bellone, who had made a move a little earlier. He caught the leader quickly and went on to the finish to win alone. A Frenchman had won on 14 July, the country's national day. He gained 55 seconds on Van Impe and 1m 06secs on Merckx. The Belgian took note: 'I will have to keep an eye on this Thévenet from now on.'

Eddy Merckx

1971

Spain's Luis Ocaña looked like he was on the way to beating Eddy Merckx when he crashed in the Pyrenees with the yellow jersey on his shoulders. That opened the way for the Belgian to claim a third victory

Thévenet, Ocaña and Merckx (above); Ocaña, Merckx, Poulidor (below): the Belgian is constant as his rivals come and go

UNFINISHED SYMPHONY

→ Was Eddy Merckx going to be beaten? Luis Ocaña had certainly thrown down the gauntlet. On the 11th stage from Grenoble to Orcières-Merlette, he went on the offensive and finished 8m 42secs ahead of Merckx, who was third. However, on the very next stage, The Cannibal attacked right from the start, and 251km later he regained 1m 56secs on Ocaña.

After a time-trial narrowly won by Merckx ahead of Ocaña, the race entered the Pyrenees with the Spaniard leading the Belgian by 7m 23secs. On the 14th stage between Revel and Luchon, a storm broke as the riders were climbing the Col de Menté. Despite the conditions, Merckx attacked once and then again without managing to drop Ocaña. The descent was more like a rushing stream, with mud and gravel making it even more dangerous. Yet again, though, Merckx was prepared to risk everything. He fell, got back in the saddle and set off again without looking back. Behind, Ocaña had also crashed in an attempt to avoid Merckx, but had then been hit by Zoetemelk and Agostinho. The impact left him unconscious and when he came round he was in the hospital at Saint-Gaudens. His Tour was over.

MERCKX REWARDS GUIMARD

→ The previous year, Eddy Merckx had not appreciated the fact that Cyrille Guimard had taken Luis Ocaña's side by refusing to work with the Belgian in the Alps before helping the Spaniard on the stage to Marseille. Merckx had then done all he could to prevent Guimard taking the green jersey by securing that prize for himself. This year, following the conclusion of the 59th Tour on La Cipale track, the Belgian, who had just won for the fourth year in succession, was keen to hand over the points title trophy he'd just won to the Frenchman: 'It is you who deserves this green jersey. It ought to be given to you.' Standing next to him, Guimard, overcome with emotion, covered his eyes with a tissue as he cried.

Eddy Merckx loved to win. But more than

1972

There was no chance of revenge for Luis Ocaña, who once again fell in the Pyrenees and abandoned in the Alps. In his absence, Cyrille Guimard emerged as Eddy Merckx's main threat as he wrapped up a fourth title

Eddy Merckx

anything he loved to be involved in a battle. And Guimard gave him one for both the yellow and the green jerseys until he was forced to abandon just two days from the finish due to agonising tendinitis. At that point he had been lying second overall, and the two men had swapped the yellow jersey back and forth between them for the whole race. The 25-year-old Frenchman

had beaten the sprinters at Saint-Brieuc and Royan, but more surprisingly than that he had staggered the great Merckx by following him in the mountains and even managing to beat him at Aix-les-Bains and on the summit of Mont Revard. It was some performance – almost as good as the Belgian's – as Merckx took six stages and a fourth title.

Luis Ocaña

In the absence of Merckx, Luis Ocaña dominated Van Impe (hidden), Thévenet, Zoetemelk and Fuente (from left to right)

1973

In the absence of Eddy Merckx, Luis Ocaña finally claimed the Tour title ahead of Bernard Thévenet. As for Raymond Poulidor, once again he appeared to be ill-fated

POULIDOR'S NEAREST MISS

→ In 1964, Raymond Poulidor missed out on taking the yellow jersey from Jacques Anquetil by just 14 seconds on the summit of the Puy de Dôme. In 1965 he failed to relieve Felice Gimondi of it by 35 seconds on the Ventoux. In 1967, he missed out on it by six seconds in the Tour's first prologue time-trial. Six years later, Poulidor's ongoing quest took an even crueller turn. At Scheveningen in the Netherlands, where the Tour started, local hero Joop Zoetemelk took victory in the 7.1km prologue, beating Poulidor by a margin of just eight-tenths of a second. It had already seemed apparent that Poulidor would never win the Tour de France. This time, he fell and was badly injured. But it now seemed likely that he would never wear the yellow jersey either – not even for a single day in his 14 Tour appearances.

1974

Just as he had done in 1970, Eddy Merckx took eight stage wins as he crushed his rivals, winning his fifth title ahead of Raymond Poulidor

FIRST STOP IN BRITAIN

→ On 29 June, the Tour de France crossed the Channel for its first-ever stage in Britain. It was a failure. As there was little culture of road racing in Britain, the authorities in Plymouth simply closed a section of dual carriageway, creating a 12km circuit that the riders covered 14 times. Dutchman Henk Poppe won the bunch sprint, while Belgium's Joseph Bruyère, Eddy Merckx's loyal lieutenant, kept the yellow jersey. But the event was greeted with almost total indifference. Twenty years later, the British federation offered an apology for that initial encounter with the Tour, saying there was 'no culture, no promotion, no publicity caravan: England wasn't ready for it.' That same evening, the race entourage took the boat back to France.

Plymouth A 38

Thévenet (here in front of Merckx and Van Impe) led the way in the 1975 Tour. As for the Belgian five-time champion, he was more victim than vanquished

1975

Unbeaten on the Tour de France, Eddy Merckx's image of invincibility finally crumbled in the face of a brilliant performance by Bernard Thévenet, who was crowned on the Champs-Élysées

Bernard Thévenet

THE KING IS DETHRONED

At the end of the 14th stage, just 150 metres from the summit of the Puy de Dôme, Eddy Merckx was chasing after Lucien Van Impe and Bernard Thévenet when a spectator jumped out of the crowd and punched him in the abdomen. The Belgian felt the blow and struggled up to the finish, apparently short of breath. Van Impe regained 49 seconds on him and Thévenet 34, but that wasn't the most serious damage. The incident impacted on Merckx hugely, who was left with a big bruise and a blow to his morale. After recovering for a few minutes, he got back onto his bike and went back down the road to find his assailant, who had already been detained by two policemen. The man would end up being fined that autumn. 'I feel sickened,' Merckx said. 'But that is the fault of this man, not the French public. There are idiots everywhere.'

On the following stage, the 15th, he would lose the yellow jersey to Thévenet on the road up to Pra-Loup. On the 17th stage he fell, injuring his hip and knee and fracturing his cheekbone. But, driven on by his courage, he refused to abandon and finished second in Paris. He was as big in defeat as he always had been in victory.

The isolated act of one idiot attacking Eddy Merckx cannot overshadow the exemplary behaviour of the millions of spectators who pack the sides of the road at the Tour each year

THE TOUR'S FANS

→ It's estimated that around 15 million people watch the Tour each year, give or take a few hundred thousand. Let's face it, it's not that easy to count them very precisely.

The Tour de France is not only the greatest moving spectacle in the world, it's also the only one of such a duration that is entirely free. You don't need to buy a ticket or acquire rights to be able to see the publicity caravan and then the peloton pass by – not even if you want to watch the stage finishes.

Immeasurable numbers of spectators descend on the Tour route. Whether in organised groups or with their families, they can spend hours awaiting the arrival of the riders, particularly on the big mountain stages. Because the peloton gets split apart there, the spectacle lasts for much longer.

These days, the relationship between the champions and the fans is harmonious. The age when nails would be scattered on the course to favour one rider or team is long gone. Nowadays, fans have respect and admiration for all the Tour's competitors.

Sadly, there are still incidents involving spectators on the race, some of them fatal. The last ones date back to 2000 and 2002, and involved vehicles in the publicity caravan, and to 2009, when a woman was knocked over by a motorcyclist from the Republican Guard. Are tragic events of this kind inevitable when a cavalcade of vehicles passes through a crowd of 15 million spectators? They are at least very rare.

Roadside slopes look like grandstands, the rain-jackets almost like tiles on a roof... Nothing would prevent fans from coming out to watch the Tour de France pass by, even the fact they have to wait for hours before seeing the peloton

Like Moses parting the Red Sea, Thévenet (up ahead) and Poulidor (number 11) must split an ocean of fans on Bastille Day as they head for Serre-Chevalier on the 16th stage of the 1975 Tour de France

Yellow is a popular choice for greeting the peloton. However, it's not the only one: there is always plenty of colour within the crowds – and sometimes even regional costumes – which all adds to the spectacle

Whether regional (Breton or Basque, for example) or national, flags flourish like some kind of strange roadside foliage that appears when the Tour passes

1976

Three veterans of the peloton finished on the podium during a year of transition at the Tour. Little Belgian climber Lucien Van Impe took advantage to stand on top of the pile

Trapped between team-mates Poulidor and Zoetemelk, Lucien Van Impe attempts to impose himself despite his diminutive stature. At the finish, he would have the last laugh together with his compatriot in the green jersey, Freddy Maertens

Lucien Van Impe

BELGIUM WINS WITHOUT MERCKX

Two Belgian riders were needed to replace Eddy Merckx, who was absent in 1976. But they performed the task particularly well. To begin with, young Freddy Maertens, 24 and a Tour de France debutant, won the prologue and then the first stage the next day. His domain of choice had been defined: he went on to win another two time-trials and four more bunch sprints. In total, Maertens captured eight stage wins, equaling the record held by Charles Pélissier (in 1930) and Eddy Merckx (1970 and 1974). As he also claimed six other top-three finishes, he was the unquestioned winner of the green jersey for the points competition.

And what about the yellow jersey? Maertens spent nine days in it and when he released it was to one of his compatriots, Lucien Van Impe. He didn't have the same profile as Maertens and, soon to turn 30, he was riding his eighth Tour. His directeur sportif, Cyrille Guimard, managed to convince him that he could target more than the King of the Mountains prize, which he had already won three times. Van Impe listened and followed the advice of Guimard the master tactician to the letter. He won the title ahead of two old campaigners: Joop Zoetemelk, who was second for third time, and Raymond Poulidor, who was third at the age of 40.

THE PRICE OF COURAGE

→ He went to the limit of his reserves, and then undoubtedly surpassed them. Half an hour after climbing onto the podium, Bernard Thévenet was still reeling. He had to be helped up the few steps leading to room 21 in the Hotel Le Christina. It had been a hellish day. The occasion was the 17th stage from Chamonix to Alpe-d'Huez, and race leader Thévenet faced danger from several angles.

There was Dietrich Thurau, lying second overall at 11 seconds, but the German blew up, losing 11m 41secs to the Frenchman. Then there was Lucien Van Impe, lying third at 33 seconds. The Belgian tried everything before cracking, finishing 1m 25secs back. Joop Zoetemelk was also in the frame, lying fifth, but he lost

3m 59secs on the final climb. Finally, there was Hennie Kuiper, who was fourth at 49 seconds: the in-form Dutchman took flight, but Thévenet went to the limits of his courage to limit his losses to 41 seconds. In the overall standings, he now led by just eight seconds. By Paris, he had pushed his advantage up to a whole 48 seconds.

1977

Two years on from his victory over Eddy Merckx, Bernard Thévenet defeated Dutchman Henni Kuiper, edging him out by a mere 48 seconds

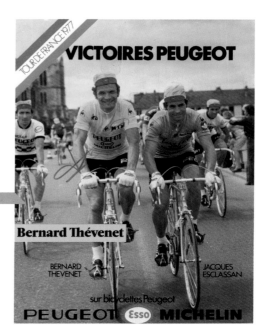

TOUR DE FRANCE 1977
VICTOIRES PEUGEOT

Bernard Thévenet

BERNARD THEVENET JACQUES ESCLASSAN

sur bicyclettes Peugeot

PEUGEOT Esso MICHELIN

1978

23-year-old Breton Bernard Hinault made a real mark on his debut, for his leadership as much as for his physical qualities. The peloton had a new 'patron'

Bernard Hinault

STRIKE IN THE PELOTON

→ Having arrived at Pla d'Adet exhausted, the riders had to get back on the road to Tarbes, location for the next day's start, and finally got to bed at 11pm. This upset the peloton, where the word went around: go slow to demonstrate your unhappiness.

Some riders tried to profit from this by escaping, but they were caught and brought back to order by a Tour debutant who displayed natural authority – French champion Bernard Hinault. The rest of the stage was completed at a slow procession, until the riders reached a point 100 metres from the finish in Valence d'Agen. There they stopped and refused to budge. The organisers, who were accused of boosting the marketability of the race to the detriment of the riders, were forced to annul this half-stage.

Hinault stamped his authority over the rest of the race, too, claiming victory at his first attempt.

DUEL ON THE CHAMPS-ELYSÉES

→ Setting out from Perreux, the final stage would put the seal on an outstanding success for Bernard Hinault. He had dominated the race: winner of four time-trials, he had brought the climbers to heel at Pau and, on the penultimate day, had even come out on top in a bunch sprint at Nogent-sur-Marne. With six stage wins already, he was leading the points classification. In the overall standings, Joop Zoetemelk was lying second at only 3m 07secs, but everyone else was at least 24 minutes down.

Despite this, the Dutchman still believed he had a chance. On the Côte de l'Homme Mort at Jouy-en-Josas, Zoetemelk attacked. Hinault followed him, then counter-attacked as the race's two dominant riders went away in the most improbable of escapes. On the Champs-Élysées, the public could scarcely believe it. The two men finished 2m 18secs ahead of a stunned peloton. Hinault won the stage, while Zoetemelk received a 10-minute penalty after testing positive for a steroid. But what a finale!

1979

Nobody could resist the fantastic Bernard Hinault, who won for the second year in succession even though veteran Joop Zoetemelk challenged him all the way to the finish

Bernard Hinault

Joop Zoetemelk

1980

Dutchman Joop Zoetemelk had to wait until his 10th Tour de France before finally topping the podium at the age of 33 after finishing second on so many occasions

STANDING THE TEST OF TIME

→ He had finished second behind Eddy Merckx in 1970 and 1971, second again behind Lucien Van Impe in 1976, and yet again to Bernard Hinault in 1978 and 1979. He would end up there again behind the Frenchman as runner-up for a sixth time in 1982. Even more so than Raymond Poulidor, who had eight podium finishes but only finished on the second step on three occasions, Joop Zoetemelk was 'the eternal second' of the Tour de France.

A multi-talented rider, who was an excellent rouleur and climber, the Dutchman suffered because he was not attack-minded. Although he won in 1980, it was undoubtedly because Hinault had been forced to quit in Pau when in the yellow jersey after suffering with tendinitis in his knee for several days. Zoetemelk moved into the yellow jersey and his Ti-Raleigh team, which was a well-drilled machine, protected him all the way into Paris. It was a victory based on merit rather than panache.

Joop Zoetemelk, Lucien Van Impe and Bernard Hinault (from left to right) move to the front as the road starts to climb. They were experienced men who knew each other well

1981

It was a year the champions returned: the majestic Bernard Hinault won his third Tour de France, while Freddy Maertens was reborn with five stage victories and the green jersey

Bernard Hinault

AUSTRALIA EMERGES

→ Besides France, up to this point only nine countries had seen one of their riders lead the overall classification, even if only for a short space of time: Switzlerand (who first had that honour in 1904), Belgium (1909), Luxembourg (1909), Italy (1912), Austria (1931), Germany (1932), the Netherlands (1951), Spain (1955) and Great Britain (1962). The 10th member of that exclusive club would be a lot further afield. By finishing third on the fifth stage between Saint-Gaudens and Saint-Lary-Soulan, right on the wheel of Bernard Hinault, Australia's Phil Anderson, a 23-year-old

Peugeot rider from Melbourne, gave a new continent a taste of yellow.

The Breton was not happy: 'He didn't want to collaborate. That is not worthy of a champion.' No matter: Anderson had the yellow jersey. The next day he finished third in the time-trial, 30 seconds behind Hinault, to whom he ceded the lead by a mere 13 seconds. The adventure fired up the Australian. The following year he would wear the yellow jersey for nine days following his victory on the ninth stage in Nancy (which just happened to be the first by an Australian) and would finish fifth in Paris.

1982

A fourth success for Bernard Hinault, who dominated a trio of Dutch riders: Joop Zoetemelk, Johan Van der Velde and Peter Winnen. Notably, the Breton won both the prologue and the final stage

Bernard Hinault

The incredible Hinault gets involved in the sprint on the Champs-Élysées and finds himself mixing it with the peloton's leading specialists – Van der Poel, Bertin, Pevenage, De Wolf – just to underline his panache

HINAULT'S PARISIAN PANACHE

He had already wrapped up his fourth Tour, crushing his rivals in the time-trials, mastering them in the mountains and controlling them on the flat. Bernard Hinault did not have a comparable rival, and because of that some observers criticised him.

As he had got older, Hinault had become more economical with his efforts. The riders were approaching the end of the sixth and final 6km lap on the Champs-Élysées. The leader, sitting on the wheel of the previous year's winner in Paris, the Belgian Pol Verschuere,

launched his sprint from a long way out. The Breton wasn't the best sprinter, but he was the freshest and the strongest. Behind him he left Adrie Van der Poel, Yvon Bertin, Rudy Pevenage and Fons De Wolf, all specialists in this kind of finale, as well as the rest of the pack.

Was it a show of panache? 'Call it what you will,' he replied. 'It's a beautiful victory. As for panache, I believe I've already shown that. Let's just say that I was making a little bit of a point.' He didn't need to do so to win the title and achieve his first Giro-Tour double.

Laurent Fignon

Pascal Simon, racked with pain, abandons (right). Laurent Fignon takes on the responsibility of leading the race and holds on to win

1983

At the end of the drawn-out agony suffered by yellow jersey Pascal Simon, a 23-year-old debutant won in Paris. Nevertheless, Laurent Fignon fully deserved his success

SIMON AT THE CROSSROADS

At the start of the 11th stage in Bagnères-de-Luchon, Pascal Simon was smiling. He was wearing the yellow jersey he had taken the day before and was sharing a joke with Laurent Fignon, who was in the white jersey of best young rider and lying second overall at 4m 22secs. With Hinault absent, the outsiders were having a ball, as the favourites for the title had all but faded out of view.

But 40km down the road, Simon crashed and fractured his shoulder-blade. He managed to get back on his back and make it to the finish. This seemed heroic, but it was only the start. Simon suffered like a martyr for a week until the 17th stage, the first major rendezvous in the Alps, where he finally abandoned with the yellow jersey still on his shoulders. He was by then only 40 seconds ahead of Fignon, who hadn't dared attack him. He had taken some time back on the Puy de Dôme, where he had been obliged to respond to attacks made by riders further down the classification in order to defend his own position. Set free after Simon's exit, Fignon wore the yellow jersey for the rest of the race.

1984

Victorious in three time-trials and a superb winner of a mountain stage, Laurent Fignon retained the title and he did so by beating his former team leader, Bernard Hinault

Laurent Fignon

YOUTH WITHOUT PITY

The young can be cruel. On the 17th stage, between Grenoble and Alpe-d'Huez, Bernard Hinault, who was trailing Laurent Fignon by 2m 46secs in the overall classification, gave all he had left. He attacked, was reeled back in, then attacked again on the flat before heading onto the climb up to Alpe-d'Huez. 'When I saw him go clear, I laughed to myself,' Fignon commented at the stage finish, where he had gained another 2m 55secs over Hinault.

This was an exceptional stage for more than one reason, because it was won – and this was a first – by a South American rider. Twenty-three-year old Luis 'Lucho' Herrera (right) was taking part in his first Tour as a member of the amateur Colombia team. He would win three Tour stages and two King of the Mountains titles (1985 and 1987) in a Tour de France that was gaining an increasingly international aspect.

BREATHLESS HINAULT WINS AGAIN

→ Bernard Hinault was in yellow, but not feeling his best. He wasn't tired because he'd taken another Giro victory, but because he simply couldn't breathe. In the Cours Fauriel in Saint-Étienne, at the end of the 14th stage, the Breton collided with Phil Anderson in the final sprint and fell heavily. With his face bloodied, he finally got onto a new bike to cross the line slowly. The diagnosis was a fracture at the base of his nose, so for the last few days he had to breathe through his mouth, caught bronchitis and was weakened by both the illness and the medication. On the climb to Luz-Ardiden (stage

1985

A Tour starting in Brittany was almost certain to end up victory for Bernard Hinault, who joined Anquetil and Merckx as a five-time winner. But it was hard going…

17), he struggled and only hung on to the yellow jersey because his team-mate Greg LeMond didn't cooperate with the attacks made by their rivals. He finished in Paris 1m 42secs up on the American – and in his debt.

Bernard Hinault

1986

A favour returned? Greg LeMond became the first American to win the Tour, thanks to the help he received from Bernard Hinault, who was crowned best climber

Greg LeMond

RETURN MATCH

→ 'In order for Greg to win, I have to have some freedom. That doesn't mean that the work I do is going to make him feel better,' Bernard Hinault said before the start. And how right he was. The Breton won the time-trial in Nantes and attacked on the first Pyrenean stage. That made him the race leader with 5m 25secs over LeMond! 'There is not the slightest problem between Greg and me,' he said.

Twenty-four hours later, the American finally took the initiative on the first stage in the Alps. The next day, the two men put on a show on the Col de la-Croix-de-Fer and the climb to Alpe-d'Huez, leaving their pursuers five minutes behind. To Hinault went the stage, the polka-dot jersey and a glorious farewell. To LeMond went victory in Paris, as predicted.

1987

Already winner of the Giro and soon to be crowned world champion, Ireland's Stephen Roche was enjoying an annus mirabilis. He won the Tour by 40 seconds from Spain's Pedro Delgado

Stephen Roche

IN THE SHADOW OF THE WALL

→ A prologue of 6km, followed the next day by a road stage of 105km and a team time-trial of 40km: just three small tests and then they would be gone. The riders grumbled about the start taking place in West Berlin, partly because of the long plane transfer that was needed to reach West Germany.

The organisers had been hoping to attract some amateur teams from the communist Eastern Bloc. But their hopes were in vain: there wasn't a single one at the start, while the German Democratic Republic refused to allow any racing on its soil, viewing the Tour's

presence in West Berlin as a provocation. The long trip east did produce some memorable images of the riders on the Kurfürstendamm (the local Champs-Élysées) and by the Brandenburg Gate, as well as beneath the wall that encircled the city. They also received an extremely warm welcome from the Berliners.

In an odd twist, at the end of the first stage, Poland's Lech Piasecki became the first rider from the Eastern Bloc to wear the yellow jersey. It was handed to him by French prime minister Jacques Chirac in the northern sector of the city, which was under French military control.

Since 1903, attempts to fine-tune the machine that is the Tour de France have been never-ending. Having the Grand Départ in West Berlin was a real achievement in organisational terms

TOUR DE FORCE

In 1903, the race's organising team comprised a handful of men. It says everything that they all managed to cram into *L'Auto*'s Cottereau, which was the only vehicle to follow the peloton… or at least it did when the riders were together!

Along the route, a few hundred armbands had been distributed to volunteers, who were quick to denounce any evidence of cheating. However, Géo Lefèvre, to whom Henri Desgrange had handed operational management of the Tour, found himself responsible for supervising random control points, putting together the list of finishers, getting all of the necessary information to Desgrange and, of course, of putting together the stage reports for the readers of *L'Auto*.

More than a century later, the statistics relating to the organisation of the Tour are staggering: it has 200 cars, 16 semi-trailers, five construction teams, a plane, broadcast crews, and about 400 people involved in nothing more than logistics. Then there is the caravan, the 50 Republican Guard motorbikes, hundreds of representatives from the forces of law and order, the medical team, the race referees and anti-doping officials, finish-line judges.

And there's the media: 2,500 journalists, photographers and consultants, 1,600 technicians and drivers covering the event for 370 papers, 120 television channels, 85 photo agencies and 70 radio stations. Every day, it's like a whole town is on the move, setting up home in one place, then taking everything down and moving again. It is the world's biggest circus, with the open sky as its big top.

The riders and officials look very stiff as they pose at a feed station in 1907 (top) and at the sign-on point in 1910, where Octave Lapize is partly hiding the figure of Henri Desgrange, while race starter Georges Abran has his flag at the ready

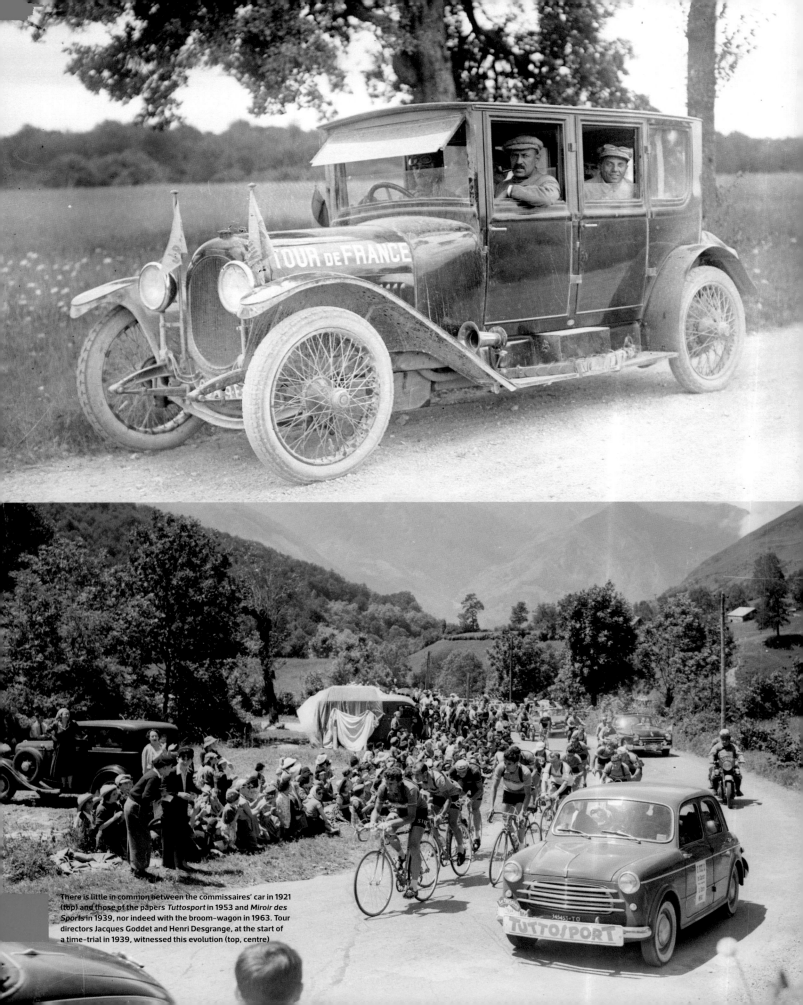

There is little in common between the commissaires' car in 1921 (top) and those of the papers *Tuttosport* in 1953 and *Miroir des Sports* in 1939, nor indeed with the broom-wagon in 1963. Tour directors Jacques Goddet and Henri Desgrange, at the start of a time-trial in 1939, witnessed this evolution (top, centre)

Motorcyclists are there to protect both the riders and the spectators – as seen here with Raymond Poulidor in 1974. They have been present on the Tour since 1953

Abbot Pistre, from Noailhac in the department of Tarn, was nicknamed 'The Pope of Rugby'. However, he didn't like to miss a chance of visiting the Tour, like this one where he is seen in the company of race director Jacques Goddet

Whether it's the presentation of the 2012 Tour by race director Christian Prudhomme (top left) or of the BMC team at the Puy du Fou in 2011 (above), the Tour is all about spectacle. But the riders receive a great a great deal of care (as is the case with Cadel Evans, bottom left) and protection from danger (such as traffic islands)

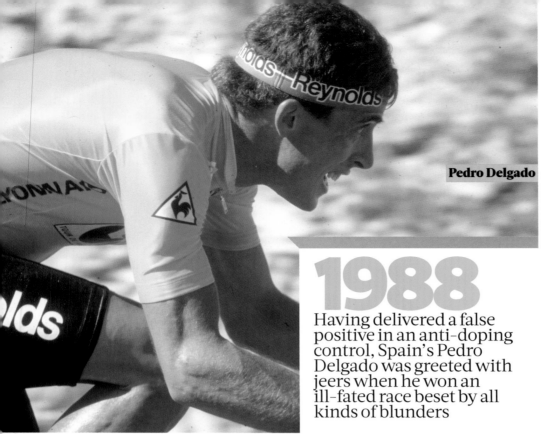

Pedro Delgado

1988

Having delivered a false positive in an anti-doping control, Spain's Pedro Delgado was greeted with jeers when he won an ill-fated race beset by all kinds of blunders

ON THE WRONG ROAD

→ The Tour's director-general, Jean-Pierre Courcol, who had succeeded Jacques Goddet, had just told Philippe Bouvatier that he would receive the same prize as the winner of the 14th stage: a Peugeot 309 Chorus. But Bouvatier was still inconsolable – having escaped early in the stage with Italy's Massimo Ghirotto and Britain's Robert Millar, the Frenchman had attacked 250 metres from the finish line at Guzet-Neige. He seemed like he might have done enough to win, until he was directed down the detour reserved for cars in the race convoy. Millar followed him, but Ghirotto took off and won the stage. 'Third on a stage will never rank as a performance,' lamented Bouvatier. The mistake made by the race commissaires deprived him of victory and he would never win a stage in the Tour.

EIGHT SECONDS!

→ Every time one rider delivered a blow, the other struck back. Greg LeMond and Laurent Fignon traded the yellow jersey between them from stage five onwards. From the start, the gap between the two men was never more than 51 seconds in Fignon's favour or 53 seconds in the American's. The night before the final time-trial of 24.5km between Versailles and Paris, Fignon's advantage of 50 seconds seemed enough to ensure he would win the race. Yet Fignon was suffering from an uncomfortable inflammation of his perineum…

At the same time, the American was using a bike more suited to time-trialling. LeMond nibbled away persistently at the deficit. At the end of 21 stages and 3,285km, he finished the Tour de France in 87 hours 38 minutes and 35 seconds, which was just eight seconds fewer than the Frenchman, who would never again come so close to winning.

Incredulity is starting to be replaced by absolute joy on the face of Greg LeMond, who has just seen on the big screen that he has won the Tour. A few minutes later, the beaten man, Laurent Fignon, is shattered

Greg LeMond

1989

The duel between Greg LeMond and Laurent Fignon finished on the Champs-Elysées with a second victory for the American by just eight minuscule seconds

1990

Having looked set for a victory 'à la Walkowiak', Italy's Claudio Chiapucci lost his grip on the yellow jersey on the penultimate days as Greg LeMond went on to claim his third overall success

The Z team, with Ronan Pensec (centre) who wore the yellow jersey during the race, raises its triumphant hero aloft. Greg LeMond has just won his third Tour, equalling Louison Bobet and Philippe Thys

Greg LeMond

THE IRON CURTAIN IS LIFTED

Olaf Ludwig's road CV was rather atypical. It featured two victories in the Peace Race (in 1982 and 1986), an event where he won a total of 38 stages over his career. He also won an Olympic gold medal in 1988 and national titles in 1978, 1986, 1989 and 1990. But what had he won as a pro? Nothing. He was 30 and making his debut at the Tour de France.

That was because he was born in Gera in East Germany, and he had spent the greater part of his sporting life on the other side of the Wall.

He had no choice until the Iron Curtain started to crumble. So belatedly he entered the world of pro cycling. He won in Besançon and took enough places of honour to secure the green jersey. These two victories would be the only ones taken by East Germany in the Tour because on 3 October 1990 Ludwig's country vanished as it unified with its neighbour to the west.

He would win two more stages for his new country: in 1992 on the Champs-Élysées and in 1993 in Montpellier.

1991

After six rather discreet performances at the Tour, the 27-year-old teammate of Pedro Delgado, Spaniard Miguel Indurain, was transformed into an awesome time-trialling and climbing machine

Miguel Indurain

Thierry Marie had previously specialised in prologues, but a brave breakaway on stage 6 put him (briefly) in the yellow jersey

METAMORPHOSIS

→ Thierry Marie had already taken three stage victories in the Tour de France, but none of them over a distance longer than 6.3km. His speciality? Prologues: he had won those in 1986 (4.6km), 1990 (6.3km) and in 1991 (5.3km). When he decided to break away on his own, 25km into the 259km sixth stage between Arras and Le Havre, he had six hours of hardship ahead of him. Even when he stretched his lead to 22 minutes with 130km remaining, he was still wondering if he had done the right thing: 'But the further I went, the less time I had to reflect on that given the degree I was suffering.' Despite being on the edge of exhaustion, he maintained a lead of 1m 54secs on the peloton and took the yellow jersey. 'Before I was dragster, now I am a marathon runner. I've proved that I know how to do everything.'

1992

A Spaniard, Miguel Indurain, took the title; a Frenchman, Laurent Jalabert, the green jersey; an Italian, Claudio Chiappucci, was the best climber. The race's roll of honour was totally befitting the European nature of the route

GAME WITHOUT FRONTIERS

→ This year's route was less like a Tour map and more like a tourist brochure. The race started at San Sebastián in Spain, visited Brussels in Belgium, Valkenburg in the Netherlands, Koblenz in Germany, then Luxembourg, before making a final exotic detour via Sestrières in Italy. There were no fewer than six countries on the menu (not including France), which stopped in Strasbourg, home of the European Parliament. In the year that the Maastricht Treaty was signed, the riders tested the idea of free circulation of people and ideas at very high speed. Miguel Indurain won the title with a record average speed of 39.504kmh. Tourism would have to wait...

Miguel Indurain

1993

As in 1992, Miguel Indurain completed the Giro-Tour double following a mighty demonstration of power that secured his third victory in succession

SUBLIME POWER

→ It had become his *modus operandi*: in the first long time-trial, Miguel Indurain would mark out his territory. In 1991, it was between Argentan and Alençon (stage 8) over 73km. He didn't win by much – just eight seconds ahead of Greg LeMond. His power was on the rise in 1992 when, over 65km in

Luxembourg (stage 9), the second-placed rider, Armand de las Cuevas, was three minutes back. On this occasion, the test was at Lac de Madine (stage 9) over 59km. The day's runner-up, Gianni Bugno, was only 2m 11secs further back.

Indurain almost seemed to excuse his performance: 'I was at the same level as in

Luxembourg, but the gaps aren't the same.' It was logical, because it was over a shorter distance. Bugno's insight was more pertinent: 'When it comes to time-trials, this guy is in a class of his own.' Whoever was right, the simple fact was that the Spaniard took the yellow jersey and no one else would come near it again.

1994

Like Eddy Merckx between 1969 and 1972, Miguel Indurain won a fourth Tour de France in succession. On this occasion Latvia's Piotr Ugrumov played second fiddle

THE BIG TURNAROUND

→ The policeman was a fan. Charged with protecting the riders from surges in the crowd as the sprint to decide the first stage of the race took place in Armentières, he stepped out to take a photo – and the result was carnage.

Wilfried Nelissen hit him head on, bringing down a host of riders. The worst affected was Laurent Jalabert, who ended up covered with blood: he suffered several fractures in his face and jaw. His Tour was over. It was thought his season was as well. In fact, just like his bike, his career had been turned upside down. Already a good rider, he was transformed, becoming the number one rider in the world (between 1995 and 1999) as he became a complete performer rather than just a sprinter. Points winner at the Tour in 1992 and 1995, he would finish as best climber in 2001 and 2002. An aggressive rider, good time-triallist and increasingly popular, he also became 'Jaja'.

Miguel Indurain

Ugrumov, Indurain and Pantani (from left to right) fill the podium. For Laurent Jalabert, however, the Tour ends on the first stage in Armentières following a very hefty crash

The peloton gather their thoughts before the stage start in Tarbes as they pause to remember Fabio Casartelli, who died the day before. On the right is his team-mate Lance Armstrong, would win in Limoges and dedicate his victory to the Italian

1995

Miguel Indurain joined Anquetil, Merckx and Hinault in the Tour de France's five-time winners' club. However, unlike that distinguished trio, the Spaniard took his victories in successive years

Miguel Indurain

A RACE IN MOURNING

On the descent of the Portet d'Aspet, at kilometre 34 on the 16th stage from Tarbes to Pau, seven riders crashed on a sharp left-hand bend. Three were quickly back on their bikes. Juan Cesar Aguirre, his shoulder badly injured, was as well but abandoned the race a few kilometres down the road. Dirk Baldinger was lifted into an ambulance, while the emergency services were trying to lift Dante Rezze back up onto the road after he had gone over the parapet into the forest below, leaving him with shock and an injury to his thigh.

As for Fabio Casartelli, he remained immobile on the road having fallen into a deep coma. His face was bloodied. His head had hit one of the concrete posts designed to prevent road-users crashing into the ravine below. His injuries were beyond treatment: he had suffered severe trauma to his head and serious brain injuries.

Transported first by ambulance and then by helicopter to hospital in Tarbes, the 24-year-old Italian died soon after arriving there.

Informed of the tragedy, the peloton rode in procession the next day and allowed the Motorola team for which the road race champion from the Barcelona Olympics had been riding to cross the line ahead of them.

A SPRINT IN THE MOUNTAINS

→ It had been scheduled to be a long stage, but it became a sprint. As a result of the fact that the Col de l'Iseran and the Galibier were covered with snow, the organisers were forced to shorten stage 9, which took the peloton to Sestrières in Italy. Instead of starting in Val d'Isère, the stage began in Monêtier-les-Bains and comprised just 46 of the 189.5km.

That was enough for Bjarne Riis to ensure that Evgeni Berzin lost the yellow jersey. The Dane attacked early and held off counters from Rominger and Indurain. He jumped to the top of the overall standings and would not be moved from it. In 2007, he confessed to having taken EPO during his career and was stripped of his title – only to be reinserted into the race's roll of honour the following year.

Bjarne Riis

1996

Looking staggeringly comfortable despite a narrow margin of victory at the finish, 32-year-old Dane Bjarne Riis ended Indurain's reign in his seventh appearance in the Tour de France

Bjarne Riis gauges the form of Miguel Indurain: the handover of power is in the process of taking place

Jan Ullrich

1997

After Denmark, Germany produced its first winner: 23-year-old Jan Ullrich beat his closest rival, Richard Virenque, by more than nine minutes

Virenque scored points, but Ullrich was only interested in the time he gained

THE POLKA-DOT KING

→ Which one of Pantani (the bronchitis-affected winner at Alpe-d'Huez and Morzine), Ullrich (the yellow jersey in Paris who was devastating in the Pyrenees and Alps) or Virenque was the Tour's best climber? It's hard to say. But one thing is for certain: as he had done in 1994, 1995 and 1996, the Frenchman won the polka-dot jersey as the King of the Mountains. He would do so again in 1999, 2003 and 2004 to set a new record.

At this point, the Frenchman had still not given up all hope of taking the overall title. With this goal in mind, he attacked on the road to Courchevel (stage 14), leading over the Glandon and the Madeleine, and dropping all of his rivals – except Ullrich. Virenque's stage victory guaranteed him second place, the best position of his career, but Ullrich took overall victory.

THE SCENT OF SCANDAL

→ Once again the Tour started on an island – the Republic of Ireland to be precise – which hosted a prologue and two stages. The Tour received a rapturous reception in the home of Stephen Roche and Sean Kelly. But this was the only good news on this Tour, because after the breath of fresh air provided by the Irish, the atmosphere on the race became very toxic.

Richard Virenque's Festina team was ejected from the race; TVM's riders (who had been taken into custody) left the race on the quiet in Switzerland; the Spanish teams also quit; a strike by the riders resulted in the cancellation of the stage between Albertville and Aix-les-Bains – and all of these incidents were directly linked to doping affairs. The race ended with Italy's Marco Pantani taking victory in Paris.

It would soon be evident why his performances were so astounding, notably those at Plateau de Beille and Les Deux-Alpes. He would be excluded from the Giro in 1999 and 2001 under suspicion of doping and died in 2004 following a cocaine overdose.

1998

Italian climber Marco Pantani completed the Giro-Tour double, but the race was severely affected by a series of doping affairs

Marco Pantani

Jan Ullrich, Marco Pantani and Bobby Julich (from left to right): the top three survivors in Paris

Ireland was the 11th country – but only the third with which France does not share a border – to host the Tour since 1906. On every occasion, the race has received an enthusiastic welcome

WHOSE TOUR IS IT ANYWAY?

→ Since the Tour's first incursion into 'foreign' territory in 1906, when it ventured to Metz, which was then part of Germany, all of the countries that share a border with France have been visited by the race at fairly regular intervals. That's also been the case for three more distant countries: the Netherlands, Great Britain and Ireland. The prize for the most Tour visits goes to Belgium, which has hosted the race on 44 occasions since 1947 – that's more than once every two years since the Second World War. The same country also stands second in the list of nations that have won the Tour with 18 victories, behind France on 36.

Most of these countries have also had the honour of hosting the start of the Tour. Listed by number of starts they are: the Netherlands, five times since 1954; Belgium, four times since 1958; Germany, three times since 1965; Switzerland, 1982; Luxembourg, twice since 1989; Spain, 1992; Ireland, 1998; Great Britain, 2007; and Monaco, 2009.

Frontiers are becoming more and more invisible. As the concept of European Union has steadily progressed, the popularity of the Tour de France has now extended beyond the borders of the country that created it. Consequently, it seems logical that the race should go and meet its fans, without it being entirely clear whether supply (on the part of the organisers) or demand (on the part of the public) came first. With the notable exception of the visit to England in 1974, all of the peloton's foreign trips have been a resounding popular success. Consequently, wherever it goes, the Tour is at home.

In 1954, the Tour started
abroad for the first time.
Amsterdam and the Netherlands
received the honour of hosting
the first foreign start

The Tour has been crossing France's borders for a long time,
heading over into Belgium in 1949 (top left) and even across the
Belgian border into Luxembourg in 1947 (bottom left), and (opposite)
going over the Spanish border in 1949 during a stage from Bordeaux
to San Sebastián and returning from San Sebastián to Pau

Setting out from Monaco in 1952 (top left), a time-trial in Barcelona in 1957 (top right with Jacques Anquetil pictured), a mountain scene in Switzerland (bottom left) and a rural setting in Ireland in 1998 (bottom right). Every style of terrain covering every era, and all were a success

Die Aktion Hermannstraße grüßt die
Tour de France

London in 2007 (top left) and West Berlin 20 years beforehand (top right) both hosted Tour starts. Dublin also hosted the start in 1998, when the stage from Enniscorthy to Cork (bottom left) enabled the Irish to witness the peloton first hand, as was the case in 2007 when the Tour headed through Kent to Canterbury (bottom right)

ROUGH PASSAGE

→ When the peloton headed onto the Passage du Gois, a 4km causeway that links the island of Noirmoutier to the French mainland and which is only passable at low tide, it was widely felt that although the Tour could not be won here, it could certainly be lost. The breeze was up, the causeway was narrow and wet, so crashes were inevitable. The big one occurred at the front of the peloton and a group of 17 riders managed to avoid it as their fallen rivals blocked the road.

The chasing group included Alex Zülle, who had finished second in 1995 and won the Vuelta in 1996 and 1997, Giro winner Ivan Gotti and Christophe Rinero and Michael Boogerd, who had finished fourth and fifth respectively in 1998. They would all lose more than six minutes on this second stage between Challans and Saint-Nazaire, and all hope of victory as well. The Armstrong show had begun.

1999

Having recovered from cancer, Lance Armstrong, previously regarded as a one-day specialist, dominated. Illegally, as it would turn out...

Lance Armstrong

2000

The 20th century drew to a close with a question hanging in the air: could anyone beat Lance Armstrong? Better than his rivals in the mountains and on the flat, the American coasted to victory

GO, MILLAR, GO!

→ Lance Armstrong stuck to his tried-and-trusted method: he blitzed the pure climbers on the first day in the mountains, which started on stage 10, and crushed the rouleurs in the time-trials. Two days from the finish, he captured his only stage victory in the test between Fribourg-en-Brisgau in Germany and Mulhouse, covering the 58.5km at an average of 53.986kmh.

The American had a stage at last after having his star billing snatched by David Millar (right) at the beginning of a Tour that didn't feature a prologue, but opened instead with a 16.5km time-trial at Futuroscope. Born in Malta, raised in Hong Kong and resident in the Basque Country, the 23-year-old Scot was taking part in his first Tour. That evening, and for the next three days, he was in yellow.

2001

A third success for Lance Armstrong, a sixth green jersey for Germany's Erik Zabel and one of the Simon brothers got an honourable mention as well. Was it just business as usual? Not for Laurent Jalabert, who provided something different by winning the polka-dot jersey

Lance Armstrong

THE SIMON SAGA

→ How was it possible that a rider who had finished 29th at Alpe-d'Huez, 10m 20secs behind stage winner Lance Armstrong, could take the yellow jersey with a comfortable advantage of 20m 07secs on the American in the overall standings? To get the answer to that question you have to go back two days to the 8th stage between Colmar and Pontarlier. Fourteen riders escaped and built up an unbelievable lead. The group split but the first four riders still finished 35m 54secs up on the peloton, while nine others came in 33m 22secs up on the main group. Among them was Stuart O'Grady, who took the yellow jersey, and François Simon, who moved into second place overall and relished what was to come. As the Australian tended to be a regular member of the *gruppetto* (those riders who get dropped and gather together to share the work heading towards the finish), the Frenchman knew that he would overtake him as soon as the road went up.

That was what happened at Alpe-d'Huez. Eighteen years after his brother Pascal, François Simon also wore the yellow jersey and held it for three days. His two other brothers, Régis and Jérôme, had to be content with winning a stage in 1985 and 1988, respectively.

Lance Armstrong

2002

After Alex Zülle in 1999 and Jan Ullrich in 2000 and 2001, it was Spaniard Joseba Beloki's turn to finish behind Lance Armstrong. Once again, the American was a drug-fuelled class apart

THE TOUR OF HONOUR

Unlucky on his first two stage-winning attempts on the Pyrenean stages – which were both won by Lance Armstrong – Laurent Jalabert tried his luck again between Lavelanet and Béziers. He had been on the attack for 429km in just three days, which was the reason why the Frenchman boosted his lead in the King of the Mountains competition. It was also why Jalabert was loved by the fans: it was because he wanted, as he put it, 'to give some happiness back to those who have given me so much'.

During the rest day, the darling of the fans announced he was going to retire at the end of the season. From that point on, the Tour's roads abounded with signs, banners and notices bearing the same message: 'Thanks Jaja'.

At 33, Jalabert carried off a second King of the Mountains title. He shares with Eddy Merckx and Bernard Hinault the honour of having won both the points classification (1992, 1995) and the mountains competition (2001, 2002).

Considered a sprinter until his terrible crash at Armentières in 1994, Laurent Jalabert transformed himself into breakaway specialist and climber. He didn't worry Armstrong, but did earn his admiration

2003

The 90th Tour de France marked the race's centenary. This appeared to motivate Jan Ullrich, who pushed Lance Armstrong all the way to the finish as the American targeted a fifth success

Lance Armstrong

Armstrong (in yellow) and Ullrich didn't give a lot of thought to nostalgia, even during what was the centenary Tour

LOOKING BACK TO THE START

Sixty riders took to the start of the first Tour de France on 1 July 1903. A hundred years later, 198 set out. In that first race the riders had six stages ahead of them, covering a total of 2,248km. The best of the 21 survivors, Maurice Garin, covered them at an average of 25.679kmh. In 2003, Lance Armstrong would lead in the 146 other finishers after covering 3,426km in 20 stages at an average of 40.940kmh.

These two events had nothing in common apart from their name and the fact that, on 6 July 2003, the start point of the first stage was the Au Réveil Matin auberge at Montgeron, which was still in good nick. An Australian, Bradley McGee, was in yellow coming out of the prologue and an American would win the title in Paris. Cycling had developed an international aspect and the Tour had become its blue riband event.

2004

Lance Armstrong claimed five of the final eight stages to win easily once again. In addition, the fans became aware of a young Frenchman called Voeckler

Lance Armstrong

VOECKLERMANIA

On the fifth stage between Amiens and Chartres, five riders put on a show and finished 12m 33secs up on the peloton. Australia's Stuart O'Grady won the sprint, but it was Frenchman Thomas Voeckler who moved to the top of the overall standings, with an advantage of 9m 35secs on Lance Armstrong, who was lying sixth. He was 25, good looking and a refreshingly straight talker, as well as being blessed with a personality where his enthusiasm was combined with humility. The French fans fell in love with their national champion, who fought to hang on to the yellow jersey for 10 days, defending it with particular courage in the Pyrenees. Voeckler couldn't know it then, but he would have a similar experience in 2011, only ceding the jersey to the favourites at the end of the 19th stage and going on to finish fourth in Paris. Once again, the public affection for him was very evident.

Lance Armstrong won the race, while Thomas Voeckler won the hearts of the fans. The Tour smiled on both men

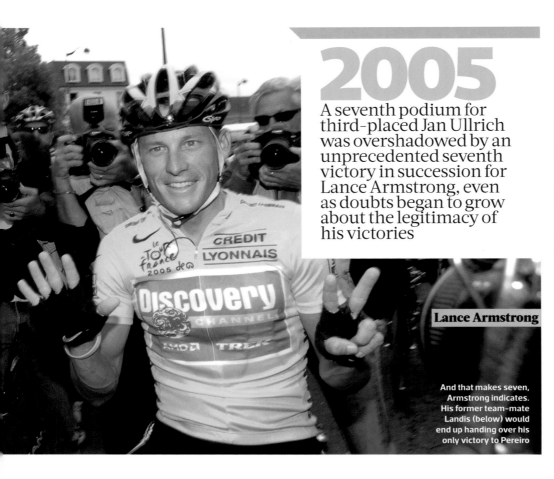

2005

A seventh podium for third-placed Jan Ullrich was overshadowed by an unprecedented seventh victory in succession for Lance Armstrong, even as doubts began to grow about the legitimacy of his victories

Lance Armstrong

And that makes seven, Armstrong indicates. His former team-mate Landis (below) would end up handing over his only victory to Pereiro

THE SEVENTH MADE US WONDER

'I would like to deliver a message to those who don't believe in cycling, to the cynics, to the sceptics. I feel sorry for you. I'm sorry you can't dream big and I'm sorry you don't believe in miracles,' declared Lance Armstrong as he stood on the podium having won his seventh Tour. It was the last one. He understood that, after so many years, suspicion was growing around him. At the time, it seemed the race's fans were more relieved to hear about his retirement after such cold domination than they were to recognise what he had achieved. 'I am not here to make friends – I am here to win,' he said. He won very effectively, but rarely won everyone over, earning instead admiration at best and questions about his methods at worst. A few weeks later, French daily *L'Équipe* would reveal that, thanks to new methods of analysis, EPO had been detected in his urine samples from the 1999 Tour. A little over seven years on, he would be making a very public confession that his success wasn't a 'miracle' after all.

A BELATED SUCCESS

This was a crazy Tour, where unexpected repercussions were the order of the day. On 14 July, Oscar Pereiro – 10th in the 2004 and 2005 Tours, and also later on in 2007 – was almost 29 minutes down on leader Floyd Landis following a bad day in the Pyrenees. The next day, he was 1m 29secs up on the American following a long-range break that went all the way to the finish on stage 13. On 17 July, at Alpe-d'Huez, the American reasserted himself in the lead by just 10 seconds. He foundered on 18 July, falling 8m 08secs behind Pereiro overall, was revitalised on 19 July and moved back to just 30 seconds in arrears and finally won in Paris on 22 July thanks to his performance in the time-trial that put him 57 seconds ahead of Pereiro.

But there was little time for celebration. Three days later, Landis, a former team-mate of Lance Armstrong, was disqualified for doping. After many hearings, Pereiro was declared the winner on 21 September 2007.

Oscar Pereiro

2006

When he crossed the finish-line in Paris, Spain's Oscar Pereiro wasn't expecting to be declared the winner of the Tour one day. But that turned out to be the case more than a year after the race had been run

2007

Almost unbelievably three riders finished within 31 seconds of each other. Alberto Contador won, beating Cadel Evans by 23 seconds and Levi Leipheimer by 31 at the end of another incident-hit Tour

Alberto Contador

BAD BEHAVIOUR

→ The 189 starters signed a 'rider's commitment to a new cycling', which was put together by the International Cycling Union (UCI) and was designed to prevent issues related to doping. Yet still the Dane Michael Rasmussen, who had held the yellow jersey for 10 days, was sent home by his team, having evaded two random dope controls in May and June. Then Alexander Vinokourov, winner of the 13th and 15th stages, tested positive for a blood transfusion. Three other riders also got caught up in the anti-doping net. As for the eventual winner, Alberto Contador, he never looked at ease.

It wasn't all bad news. The start, which took place in London, was an extraordinary success. All of the major sights in the capital made appearances – Big Ben, Buckingham Palace, Westminster Abbey, Tower Bridge, Trafalgar Square – and the riders were cheered on by immense crowds. After the failure of 1974, Great Britain was growing to love the Tour de France.

Moreau, Soler, Contador, Boonen, Txurruka (from left to right), the survivors of a strange Tour. In London, everything seems to be going perfectly

MARATHON MAN

Carlos Sastre first lined up in the Tour of Italy in 1999, in the Tour of Spain in 2000 and in the Tour de France in 2001. Following that, and right to the end of his career on 15 September 2011, he lined up in two grand tours every season: he doubled up at the Tour and Vuelta on six occasions and the Giro and Tour twice. And twice, in 2006 and 2010, he lined up at the start of the Giro, Tour and Vuelta in the same year.

In total, that was 28 grand tours, and he showed remarkable consistency: he finished in the top 10 on 15 occasions. Everyone was delighted to see him win on the Champs-Élysées in 2008, as it seemed a fitting reward for his whole career. Attentive at the start of the race, prudent in the Pyrenees, the 33-year-old Spaniard attacked on the climb up to Alpe-d'Huez in order to put some distance between himself and Cadel Evans, who was threatening the yellow jersey of Sastre's team-mate, Fränk Schleck. The tactic paid off: he won the stage and took the yellow jersey. Justice had been done.

At 33, Carlos Sastre reaches the summit of his career and discovers the pleasure of signing autographs

Carlos Sastre

2008

Another Spanish victory: after Pereiro and Contador, 33-year-old Carlos Sastre reaped the reward of an exemplary career and the subtle tactical games of his team

Alberto Contador

Lance Armstrong leads Alberto Contador. Team-mates? It seems so. Friends? Not in the least. Events during the race proved that

2009

Lance Armstrong once again attempted to push the limits of the possible, but on this occasion came up against someone who was stronger than him: his team-mate Alberto Contador, who claimed his second title

BROTHERS IN ARMS

Mark Cavendish continued to amass stage victories (he would end up with six), and the Schleck brothers (with Andy second in Paris and Fränk fifth) continued to look out for one another rather than focus on the yellow jersey. Nobody really noticed the pair of them. The real duel in this Tour pitched 26-year-old Contador against his 'team-mate' at Astana. Back in the sport after three years away from competition, Lance Armstrong was set on conquering the Tour for an eighth time at the age of almost 38.

The Texan was kidding himself, even though he missed out on the yellow jersey by just 22 hundredths of a second, having caught the Spaniard out on the third stage. But Contador responded with some key blows before delivering his final thrust in the Alps. 'I've had some difficult moments,' he admitted after the 15th stage, Verbier, where he took the yellow jersey. This was seen as a dig at Armstrong, who would finish third in Paris, 5m 24secs down.

FIGHTING FOR NO REASON

→ On the 15th stage between Pamiers and Bagnères-de-Luchon, which was won by Thomas Voeckler, Andy Schleck attacked. High on the Port de Balès with 25km to the finish, he was going away from Alberto Contador – but then stopped when his chain unshipped. The Spaniard passed him and, at the finish, Contador had taken Schleck's yellow jersey by finishing 39 seconds ahead of him. The same gap would separate the two men in Paris.

That was the key turning point in a Tour where the two main contenders, friends away from the bike, spoke a good deal, but didn't provide as much action. Everyone was left wanting more. And it was that desire for more that would end up costing Contador. On 30 September he was suspended by the UCI: traces of clenbuterol had been found in a urine sample he gave in Pau. His defence? Unwitting ingestion of the product in a contaminated steak.

Following a final appeal hearing, Contador would finally be condemned in February 2012 and penalised with a retroactive ban, while Schleck was declared the winner.

Alberto Contador

The image is misleading. The rightful yellow jersey is in fact Andy Schleck and not Alberto Contador, who is tracking him here and who will later be disqualified for doping

2010

The race was dominated by the duel between Alberto Contador and Andy Schleck. The Spaniard won it by just 39 seconds, only to be disqualified for doping a year and a half later

2011

Australia joined the 11-strong list of countries that have won the Tour thanks to 34-year-old veteran Cadel Evans, who had already finished second in 2007 and 2008. His seventh attempt turned out perfectly

Droopy smiles at last: second in 2007 and 2008, Australian Cadel Evans, 34, savours the joy of victory with his directeur sportif, John Lelangue

Cadel Evans

AN ALL-TERRAIN CHAMPION

→ Phil Anderson, the first Australian to wear in the yellow jersey (1981) and the first to win a stage (1982), inspired his compatriots, who had shone on the Tour for a decade. Stuart O'Grady, Bradley McGee, Robbie McEwen and Cadel Evans had all at one time or another led the race. Neil Stephens, Baden Cooke and Simon Gerrans had also won stages. Even better, the Aussies had almost monopolised the green jersey thanks to Robbie McEwen, who claimed it in 2002, 2004 and 2006, and Baden Cooke, who won it in 2003.

The ultimate consecration came thanks to Cadel Evans, who won the overall title at the end of a marvellously tactical race. The former winner of the Mountain Bike World Cup (1998) maintained control over brothers Andy (second) and Fränk Schleck (third), as well as the astonishing Thomas Voeckler (fourth), to take the yellow jersey on the penultimate day in the decisive time-trial.

2012

Bradley Wiggins became the first Brit to win the Tour, with the help of compatriot and Sky team-mate Chris Froome

Bradley Wiggins

Bradley Wiggins was ably supported by his Team Sky crew on his way to Britain's first victory. Green jersey winner Peter Sagan also impressed

WIGGO!

→ Some riders compete in the Tour de France on a bike. Bradley Wiggins ate his way through the route in a train, comprising his hugely powerful Sky team, which helped him to a comfortable win in Paris.

The 32-year-old dominated the two long time-trials in a race that he himself couldn't have designed any better to maximise his chances. In the mountains his fellow Brit Chris Froome, 27, who is acknowledged as a superior climber, dutifully helped protect Wiggo and made second place safe as the duo gradually broke Vincenzo Nibali's resistance.

Elsewhere, Thomas Voeckler was the King of the Mountains, while Slovak Peter Sagan

(the green jersey winner) and Germany's André Greipel both impressed by winning three stages each. Team Sky's Mark Cavendish was less prolific than usual, only winning three stages as he kept one eye on the Olympic Road Race and concentrated on supporting Wiggins.

Of course, Britain was expected to do well in the velodrome at the Olympics, with the experience of Sir Chris Hoy and Victoria Pendleton complementing the emerging talent of Jason Kenny and Laura Trott. But by winning the Tour, the Olympic Road Time-Trial and BBC Sports Personality of the Year, Sir Bradley is living proof that Britain's love affair with road cycling is in full bloom.

TOUR WINNERS AND PODIUM FINISHERS

1903
1. Maurice GARIN (FRA, 32 years)
2. Lucien POTHIER (FRA)
3. Fernand AUGEREAU (FRA)

1904
1. Henri CORNET (FRA, 20)
2. Jean-Baptiste DORTIGNACQ (FRA)
3. Aloïs CATTEAU (BEL)

1905
1. Louis TROUSSELIER (FRA, 24)
2. Hippolyte AUCOUTURIER (FRA)
3. Jean-Baptiste DORTIGNACQ (FRA)

1906
1. René POTTIER (FRA, 27)
2. Georges PASSERIEU (FRA)
3. Louis TROUSSELIER (FRA)

1907
1. Lucien PETIT-BRETON (FRA, 25)
2. Gustave GARRIGOU (FRA)
3. Émile GEORGET (FRA)

1908
1. Lucien PETIT-BRETON (FRA, 26)
2. François FABER (LUX)
3. Georges PASSERIEU (FRA)

1909
1. François FABER (LUX, 22)
2. Gustave GARRIGOU (FRA)
3. Jean ALAVOINE (FRA)

1910
1. Octave LAPIZE (FRA, 23)
2. François FABER (LUX)
3. Gustave GARRIGOU (FRA)

1911
1. Gustave GARRIGOU (FRA, 27)
2. Paul DUBOC (FRA)
3. Émile GEORGET (FRA)

1912
1. Odile DEFRAYE (BEL, 24)
2. Eugène CHRISTOPHE (FRA)
3. Gustave GARRIGOU (FRA)

1913
1. Philippe THYS (BEL, 23)
2. Gustave GARRIGOU (FRA)
3. Marcel BUYSSE (BEL)

1914
1. Philippe THYS (BEL, 24)
2. Henri PÉLISSIER (FRA)
3. Jean ALAVOINE (FRA)

1919
1. Firmin LAMBOT (BEL, 33)
2. Jean ALAVOINE (FRA)
3. Eugène CHRISTOPHE (FRA)

1920
1. Philippe THYS (BEL, 30)
2. Hector HEUSGHEM (BEL)
3. Firmin LAMBOT (BEL)

1921
1. Léon SCIEUR (BEL, 33)
2. Hector HEUSGHEM (BEL)
3. Honoré BARTHÉLEMY (FRA)

1922
1. Firmin LAMBOT (BEL, 36)
2. Jean ALAVOINE (FRA)
3. Félix SELLIER (BEL)

1923
1. Henri PÉLISSIER (FRA, 34)
2. Ottavio BOTTECCHIA (ITA)
3. Romain BELLENGER (FRA)

1924
1. Ottavio BOTTECCHIA (ITA, 30)
2. Nicolas FRANTZ (LUX)
3. Lucien BUYSSE (FRA)

1925
1. Ottavio BOTTECCHIA (ITA, 31)
2. Lucien BUYSSE (BEL)
3. Bartolomeo AIMO (ITA)

1926
1. Lucien BUYSSE (BEL, 34)
2. Nicolas FRANTZ (LUX)
3. Bartolomeo AIMO (ITA)

1927
1. Nicolas FRANTZ (LUX, 28)
2. Maurice DEWAELE (BEL)
3. Félicien VERVAECKE (BEL)

1928
1. Nicolas FRANTZ (LUX, 29)
2. André LEDUCQ (FRA)
3. Maurice DEWAELE (BEL)

1929
1. Maurice DEWAELE (BEL, 33)
2. Giuseppe PANCERA (ITA)
3. Joseph DEMUYSÈRE (BEL)

1930
1. André LEDUCQ (FRA, 26)
2. Learco GUERRA (ITA)
3. Antonin MAGNE (FRA)

1931
1. Antonin MAGNE (FRA, 27)
2. Joseph DEMUYSÈRE (BEL)
3. Antonio PESENTI (ITA)

1932
1. André LEDUCQ (FRA, 28)
2. Kurt STOEPEL (GER)
3. Francesco CAMUSSO (ITA)

1933
1. Georges SPEICHER (FRA, 26)
2. Learco GUERRA (ITA)
3. Giuseppe MARTANO (ITA)

1934
1. Antonin MAGNE (FRA, 30)
2. Giuseppe MARTANO (ITA)
3. Roger LAPÉBIE (FRA)

1935
1. Romain MAES (BEL, 22)
2. Ambrogio MORELLI (ITA)
3. Félicien VERVAECKE (BEL)

1936
1. Sylvère MAES (BEL, 27)
2. Antonin MAGNE (FRA)
3. Félicien VERVAECKE (BEL)

1937
1. Roger LAPÉBIE (FRA, 26)
2. Mario VICINI (ITA)
3. Léo AMBERG (SUI)

1938
1. Gino BARTALI (ITA, 24)
2. Félicien VERVAECKE (BEL)
3. Victor COSSON (FRA)

1939
1. Sylvère MAES (BEL, 30)
2. René VIETTO (FRA)
3. Lucien VLAEMINCK (BEL)

1947
1. Jean ROBIC (FRA, 26)
2. Édouard FACHLEITNER (FRA)
3. Pierre BRAMBILLA (ITA)

1948
1. Gino BARTALI (ITA, 34)
2. Albéric SCHOTTE (BEL)
3. Guy LAPÉBIE (FRA)

1949
1. Fausto COPPI (ITA, 30)
2. Gino BARTALI (ITA)
3. Jacques MARINELLI (FRA)

1950
1. Ferdi KUBLER (SUI, 31)
2. Constant Stan OCKERS (BEL)
3. Louison BOBET (FRA)

1951
1. Hugo KOBLET (SUI, 26)
2. Raphaël GÉMINIANI (FRA)
3. Lucien LAZARIDÈS (FRA)

1952
1. Fausto COPPI (ITA, 33)
2. Constant Stan OCKERS (BEL)
3. Bernardo RUIZ (ESP)

1953
1. Louison BOBET (FRA, 28)
2. Jean MGERÉJAC (FRA)
3. Giancarlo ASTRUA (ITA)

1954
1. Louison BOBET (FRA, 29)
2. Ferdi KUBLER (SUI)
3. Fritz SCHAER (SUI)

1955
1. Louison BOBET (FRA, 30)
2. Jean BRANKART (BEL)
3. Charly GAUL (LUX)

1956
1. Roger WALKOWIAK (FRA, 29)
2. Gilbert BAUVIN (FRA)
3. Jan ADRIAENSSENS (BEL)

1957
1. Jacques ANQUETIL (FRA, 23)
2. Marcel JANSSENS (BEL)
3. Adolf CHRISTIAN (AUT)

1958
1. Charly GAUL (LUX, 26)
2. Vito FAVERO (ITA)
3. Raphaël GÉMINIANI (FRA)

1959
1. Federico BAHAMONTES (ESP, 31)
2. Henry ANGLADE (FRA)
3. Jacques ANQUETIL (FRA)

1960
1. Gastone NENCINI (ITA, 30)
2. Graziano BATTISTINI (ITA)
3. Jan ADRIAENSENS (BEL)

1961
1. Jacques ANQUETIL (FRA, 27)
2. Guido CARLESI (ITA)
3. Charly GAUL (LUX)

1962
1. Jacques ANQUETIL (FRA, 28)
2. Joseph PLANCKAERT (BEL)
3. Raymond POULIDOR (FRA)

1963
1. Jacques ANQUETIL (FRA, 29)
2. Federico BAHAMONTES (ESP)
3. José PEREZ FRANCES (ESP)

1964
1. Jacques ANQUETIL (FRA, 30)
2. Raymond POULIDOR (FRA)
3. Federico BAHAMONTES (ESP)

1965
1. Felice GIMONDI (ITA, 23)
2. Raymond POULIDOR (FRA)
3. Gianni MOTTA (ITA)

1966
1. Lucien AIMAR (FRA, 25)
2. Jan JANSSEN (HOL)
3. Raymond POULIDOR (FRA)

1967
1. Roger PINGEON (FRA, 27)
2. Julio JIMENEZ (ESP)
3. Franco BALMANION (ITA)

1968
1. Jan JANSSEN (HOL, 28)
2. Herman VAN SPRINGEL (BEL)
3. Ferdinand BRACKE (BEL)

1969
1. Eddy MERCKX (BEL, 24)
2. Roger PINGEON (FRA)
3. Raymond POULIDOR (FRA)

1970
1. Eddy MERCKX (BEL, 25)
2. Joop ZOETEMELK (HOL)
3. Gösta PETTERSSON (SWE)

1971
1. Eddy MERCKX (BEL, 26)
2. Joop ZOETEMELK (HOL)
3. Lucien VAN IMPE (BEL)

1972
1. Eddy MERCKX (BEL, 27)
2. Felice GIMONDI (ITA)
3. Raymond POULIDOR (FRA)

1973
1. Luis OCANA (ESP, 28)
2. Bernard THÉVENET (FRA)
3. José Manuel FUENTE (ESP)

1974
1. Eddy MERCKX (BEL, 29)
2. Raymond POULIDOR (FRA)
3. Vicente LOPEZ CARRIL (ESP)

1975
1. Bernard THÉVENET (FRA, 27)
2. Eddy MERCKX (BEL)
3. Lucien VAN IMPE (BEL)

1976
1. Lucien VAN IMPE (BEL, 30)
2. Joop ZOETEMELK (HOL)
3. Raymond POULIDOR (FRA)

1977
1. Bernard THÉVENET (FRA, 29)
2. Hennie KUIPER (HOL)
3. Lucien VAN IMPE (BEL)

1978
1. Bernard HINAULT (FRA, 24)
2. Joop ZOETEMELK (HOL)
3. Joaquim AGOSTINHO (POR)

1979
1. Bernard HINAULT (FRA, 25)
2. Joop ZOETEMELK (HOL)
3. Joaquim AGOSTINHO (POR)

1980
1. Joop ZOETEMELK (HOL, 34)
2. Hennie KUIPER (HOL)
3. Raymond MARTIN (FRA)

1981
1. Bernard HINAULT (FRA, 27)
2. Lucien VAN IMPE (BEL)
3. Robert ALBAN (FRA)

1982
1. Bernard HINAULT (FRA, 28)
2. Joop ZOETEMELK (HOL)
3. Johan VAN DER VELDE (HOL)

1983
1. Laurent FIGNON (FRA, 23)
2. Angel ARROYO (ESP)
3. Peter WINNEN (HOL)

1984
1. Laurent FIGNON (FRA, 24s)
2. Bernard HINAULT (FRA)
3. Greg LEMOND (USA)

1985
1. Bernard HINAULT (FRA, 31)
2. Greg LEMOND (USA)
3. Stephen ROCHE (IRE)

1986
1. Greg LEMOND (USA, 25)
2. Bernard HINAULT (FRA)
3. Urs ZIMMERMAN (SUI)

1987
1. Stephen ROCHE (IRE, 27)
2. Pedro DELGADO (ESP)
3. Jean-François BERNARD (FRA)

1988
1. Pedro DELGADO (ESP, 28)
2. Stephen ROOKS (HOL)
3. Fabio PARRA (COL)

1989
1. Greg LEMOND (USA, 28)
2. Laurent FIGNON (FRA)
3. Pedro DELGADO (ESP)

1990
1. Greg LEMOND (USA, 29)
2. Claudio CHIAPPUCCI (ITA)
3. Erik BREUKINK (HOL)

1991
1. Miguel INDURAIN (ESP, 27)
2. Gianni BUGNO (ITA)
3. Claudio CHIAPPUCCI (ITA)

1992
1. Miguel INDURAIN (ESP, 28)
2. Claudio CHIAPPUCCI (ITA)
3. Gianni BUGNO (ITA)

1993
1. Miguel INDURAIN (ESP, 29)
2. Tony ROMINGER (SUI)
3. Zenon JASKULA (POL)

1994
1. Miguel INDURAIN (ESP, 30)
2. Piotr UGRUMOV (LAT)
3. Marco PANTANI (ITA)

1995
1. Miguel INDURAIN (ESP, 31)
2. Alex ZÜLLE (SUI)
3. Bjarne RIIS (DEN)

1996
1. Bjarne RIIS (DEN, 32)
2. Jan ULLRICH (GER)
3. Richard VIRENQUE (FRA)

1997
1. JAN ULLRICH (GER, 23)
2. Richard VIRENQUE (FRA)
3. Marco PANTANI (ITA)

1998
1. Marco PANTANI (ITA, 28)
2. Jan ULLRICH (GER)
3. Bobby JULICH (USA)

1999
1. Lance ARMSTRONG (USA, 27)*
2. Alex ZÜLLE (SUI)
3. Fernando ESCARTIN (ESP)

2000
1. Lance ARMSTRONG (USA, 28)*
2. Jan ULLRICH (GER)
3. Joseba BELOKI (ESP)

2001
1. Lance ARMSTRONG (USA, 29)*
2. Jan ULLRICH (GER)
3. Joseba BELOKI (ESP)

2002
1. Lance ARMSTRONG (USA, 30)*
2. Joseba BELOKI (ESP)
3. Raimondas RUMSAS (LIT)

2003
1. Lance ARMSTRONG (USA, 31)*
2. Jan ULLRICH (GER)
3. Alexandre VINOKOUROV (KAZ)

2004
1. Lance ARMSTRONG (USA, 32)*
2. Andreas KLÖDEN (GER)
3. Ivan BASSO (ITA)

2005
1. Lance ARMSTRONG (USA, 33)*
2. Ivan BASSO (ITA)
3. Jan ULLRICH (GER)

2006
1. Oscar PEREIRO (ESP, 29)
2. Andreas KLÖDEN (GER)
3. Carlos SASTRE (ESP)

2007
1. Alberto CONTADOR (ESP, 24)
2. Cadel EVANS (AUS)
3. Levi LEIPHEIMER (USA)

2008
1. Carlos SASTRE (ESP, 33)
2. Cadel EVANS (AUS)
3. Bernhard KOHL (AUT)

2009
1. Alberto CONTADOR (ESP, 26)
2. Andy SCHLECK (LUX)
3. Lance ARMSTRONG (USA)

2010
1. Andy SCHLECK (LUX, 25)
2. Denis MENCHOV (RUS)
3. Samuel SANCHEZ (ESP)

2011
1. Cadel EVANS (AUS, 26)
2. Andy SCHLECK (LUX)
3. Frank SCHLECK (LUX)

2012
1. Bradley WIGGINS (GBR, 32)
2. Christopher FROOME (GBR)
3. Vincenzo NIBALI (ITA)

*Armstrong has since been stripped of these titles and these years have no official winner.

100 GREATEST MOMENTS
FROM 100 YEARS OF
THE TOUR DE FRANCE

HIT THE ROAD
WITH CYCLIST

Cyclist is the magazine for people who are passionate about road cycling. Every month, it shows the rides and sportives around Europe that should be on every cyclist's must-do list, and presents the latest gear and technology, with insights from the industry's leading experts. Stunning imagery and in-depth writing make *Cyclist* the perfect way to fill those gaps when you're not riding your bike.

Cyclist, Dennis Publishing,
30 Cleveland Street, London W1T 4JD
Web: **www.cyclistmag.co.uk**
Email: **cyclist@dennis.co.uk**

Facebook: **facebook.com/cyclistmag**

Twitter: **twitter.com/cyclistmag**

EDITORIAL
Editor **Pete Muir**
Deputy Editor **Stu Bowers**
Art Editor **Rob Milton**
Staff Writer **James Spender**
Staff Writer **Peter Stuart**
Chief Sub Editor **Michael Donlevy**
Design **Andrew Sumner**

Publisher **Nicola Bates**
Publishing Director **James Burnay**
Digital Production Manager **Nicky Baker**

ADVERTISING
Group Ad Manager **Claudia Nicoletti-Dowd**
Business Development Director **Sean Igoe**
Account Manager **Chris Stowell**
Senior Sales Executive **Andrew Marriott**

MANAGEMENT
MagBook Publisher **Dharmesh Mistry**
Operations Director **Robin Ryan**
MD of Advertising **Julian Lloyd-Evans**
Newstrade Director **David Barker**
Commercial & Retail Director **Martin Belson**
Chief Operating Officer **Brett Reynolds**
Group Finance Director **Ian Leggett**
Chief Executive **James Tye**
Chairman **Felix Dennis**

COVER IMAGE Kristof Ramon

PICTURE CREDITS
Presse Sports, Argueyroles-Presse
Sports, Biville Presse-Sports, Boutroux-
Presse Sports, Clement-Presse Sports,
Deschamps-Presse Sports, Fablet-Presse
Sports, Fel-Presse Sports, Landrain-
Presse Sports, Mantey-Presse Sports, de
Martignac-Presse Sports, Martin-Presse
Sports, Mons-Presse Sports, Mounic-Presse
Sports, Prevost-Presse Sports, Rochard-
Presse Sports, Rondeau-Presse Sports,
Sunada-Presse Sports, Collection Laget